DILEMMAS OF MODERN FAMILY LIFE

Dilemmas of Modern Family Life

edited by
Gerard Frinking
Tineke Willemsen

THESIS PUBLISHERS
AMSTERDAM 1997

ISBN 90-5170-420-8
NUGI 662/665

Contents

Preface

The contributions included in this book are based on the results of a research programme on 'Developments in the division of paid and unpaid work,' carried out in the early 1990's. The programme focuses on describing and explaining differences in the degree of participation in paid and unpaid work. Most of the participants have tailored a selection of their results to the perspective chosen in this volume.

The programme has benefited financial support from the Work and Organization Research Centre (WORC) of the Faculty of Social and Behaviourial Sciences at Tilburg University.

With the publication of this volume the editors are aiming at a large dissemination of the results of the WORC research to a broad audience of researchers and policy makers.

They are grateful for the translation service of Vickie Wightman and the technical assistance by Anita van Wallinga, who have made publication of this collection in due time possible.

Gerard Frinking   Tilburg University
Tineke Willemsen   December 1996

Introduction

Gerard Frinking

The family is once again back on the political and academic agenda. Interest in the family is particularly keen in the Netherlands. This is even apparent in the terminology used. A term like 'family policy,' which had long been banned from the parlance of policy makers and politicians, is making a triumphant comeback. This revaluation can also be observed in the scientific study of the family.

One can only guess at the reasons for this renewed interest in the family. It may result from the view that stable relationships within the nuclear family and among relatives are of crucial importance to society as a whole. There is a growing awareness that the diverse functions of the family cannot be taken over by other social institutions. The recognition of the importance of the family, in which the socialization of the individual essentially takes place, coalesces with the diminishing role of the government and the emergence of the market, two actors that also greatly influence the citizen's life in the modern welfare state.

Compared with a few decades ago, the present-day family has changed considerably, in terms of both form and content. Partly as a result of demographic factors such as the decreasing number of births, increasing cohabitation, and the rising divorce rate, a plurality of primary life styles have come into existence. In addition, the internal relations within the family have changed. The economically dominant position of the husband has weakened. The wife, in contrast, has given up her almost exclusive orientation towards the family in exchange for growing participation in the labour market. There is also a trend within the family to divide the caring tasks less unequally.

This redistribution of tasks, which has resulted from, among other things, active government intervention, has had far-reaching consequences for both the individual and society. For the individual, the straightforwardness of the traditional pre-structured pattern has been replaced by often difficult and complicated options between divergent alternatives. For society, the increased participation of women in the labour market makes it necessary to create facilities on a large scale in order to enable working parents to fulfil their caring tasks. Within a relatively short period of time, the government was confronted with the consequences of its own policies. The diminished availability of women for caring tasks in the family suddenly made society aware of the value of unpaid work. In other fields, as well, the importance of caring tasks became manifest, especially in volunteer work.

In this collection, a close look is taken at dilemmas facing the modern family when both parents wish to combine their task as educators with the duties undertaken in the labour market. The developments in the distribution of paid and unpaid work are an important starting point. The fact is that the process of labour distribution has been the catalyst in the emergence of novel relations within the family. Attention will also be paid to the way in which families weigh the pros and cons in situations that are new to them. Finally, the social context will be taken into consideration, with an emphasis on the possible influence of government policy.

The contributions included in this book are based on the results of a research programme on 'Developments in the division of paid and unpaid work,' carried out in the early 1990's. Nearly all the participants in this programme have tailored a selection of their findings, which in a number of cases are of a tentative nature, to the perspective chosen in this collection. Since the interaction between paid and unpaid work formed the core of the programme, this aspect of the research question is clearly recognisable in most contributions.

The research mainly focused on the description of the Dutch situation. This was a deliberate choice. The advantage of concentrating on one country is that the results will have greater depth and coherence than those obtained in international comparative research. The disadvantage is that the specific character of Dutch family relations stands out less clearly. In order not to ignore this aspect completely in this collection, a number of chapters contain references to situations obtaining in other European countries. Only in the first chapter, however, does this aspect receive close attention.

The purpose of this first chapter is to illustrate the position of Dutch women in the European context (with some comparisons with the USA), especially with respect to their family situation and their participation in the labour market. Tineke Willemsen shows that, in the Netherlands, the gap between attitudes and behaviours is even wider than in other countries, making this country a good place to study the causes and the consequences of this discrepancy, which can be found in a more or less weakened form in many other countries.

In Chapter 2, Ad Vossen and Jan Nelissen present the results of a time-series analysis of data concerning motherhood and paid employment. Two different time perspectives are used: longitudinal, based upon birth cohorts of women, and cross-sectional, on the basis of period observations. The data are generated by a micro-simulation model that makes it possible to establish age profiles of the phenomena in question. One profile describes a motherhood career and the other an employment career, in terms of both intensity and timing aspects. A thorough inspection of the profiles leads to the conclusion that the origin of the incompatibility between motherhood and a professional career must be traced to the beginning of the sixties, marking the start of a period during which the dilemma gradually got worse. The women in question were the first to be confronted with the problem of finding out on a large scale how to reconcile work and family. The micro-simulation reconstruction of their lives sheds new light on the choices they have finally made.

In Chapter 3, Heleen van Luijn reports the findings of a nation-wide survey among Dutch women between the ages of 20 and 40 with regard to their ambivalence towards having children. It appears that about 15 percent of the respondents are having or have had serious doubts about having children for at least one year. The analysis of the motives of these women leads to four important factors: (1) threat to independence and self-realisation; (2) material restrictions; (3) too high responsibility of raising children, and (4) unwillingness of the partner. In-depth interviews with the women in doubt revealed the existence of various sub-groups. Problems with the combination of work and family seemed to be an important category. The author attributes the origins of the ambivalence to the ongoing process of emancipation, to circumstances in the early childhoods of the women, and to the attitudes of the partner. Policy measures may have a certain impact on the decision-making for these women in removing some barriers they experience, especially in the case of working mothers.

In Chapter 4, Thérèse van den Heuvel and Monique Turkenburg consider the differences and similarities between women of various levels of education who combine a paid job with taking care of children. They look into the dilemmas these women have to face, their experiences, and their strategies with respect to the various opportunities and constraints inherent in combining motherhood with a paid job. The authors raise the question whether a change in motherhood or child care facilities are responsible for the apparent decrease in the number of (full-time) years devoted to motherhood. They nonetheless note that all these categories of women still have the main responsibility of raising their children.

Chapter 5 focuses on men, or to be more precise, on fathers in a period of transition. Are fathers really participating in the daily life of the family, and to what degree have they changed their opinions and behaviour? Suzanne Dölle, Mirjam van Dongen, and Menno Jacobs present new survey data about fatherhood. They examined several stages in the lives of men: cohabiting and childless; becoming and being a father; and fatherhood after divorce. It seems that the majority of men are not really aware of any kind of dilemma when they become fathers. However, by opting for greater and deeper involvement in child rearing or in striving to realise their conception of fatherhood by being an 'involved,' a 'visiting' or a 'distant' father after divorce, they suddenly become aware of hard choices.

In Chapter 6, Hester van der Vinne and Mascha Brink examine the observed gap between attitudes and practices concerning the division of paid and unpaid work. How do men and women view the relationship between their opinions and their practices? Do they consider this discrepancy a dilemma? Using data from a study in which 25 couples discuss, explain, and comment on their division of tasks, the authors attempt to find plausible explanations for the observed discrepancy. The interview results support three explanations: one based on lack of control over behaviour; one based on weak attitudes; and a third based on situational factors. It seems that influencing the division of labour through gender role attitudes will not be an easy task.

How will government policy in the long run affect important events in the lives of women, such as labour force participation and having children? In Chapter 7, Saskia

Keuzenkamp examines the impact of a variety of legal measures aimed at the reconciliation of work and family. The review of the available literature indicates a strong increase in the labour participation of women. However, reliable evidence on the impact on family formation was rather small. In order to get a better understanding of the combined effects of various policies, a Delphi project was set up. The panel of experts consulted expect that the three policy scenarios submitted (child care and leave policies, policies to make the organisation of paid labour more flexible and 'individualisation' policies) will only affect women who are already willing to combine work and family. Women exclusively orientated to either work or motherhood are less sensitive to the incentives provided by the measures proposed. Since not many of these women are willing to choose the 'combination' model, the effects of equality policies will not bring about major changes in their life-courses in the future. Even if the outcome of current options remains largely the same, the underlying decision-making process may possibly become less complicated.

In Chapter 8, the editors of this volume, Gerard Frinking and Tineke Willemsen, after summing up the main results of the study, sketch a general framework which may clarify how the outcome of the decision-making in families with regard to the division of paid and unpaid work is connected to a specific mode of societal 'regulation.' The question to be answered refers to the impact of social, economic, and institutional forces on the kind of dilemmas which are associated with the options men and women have to make in relation to work and family in the Dutch society, at present and in the future. The authors are pessimistic about possible changes in the division of work towards a more equal share of paid and unpaid labour in families. However, new legislation may modify the current situation, for example in changing the ideological and material profits for men and women in favour of a more balanced division of work.

1

Dutch women and men between egalitarianism and traditionality

Tineke Willemsen

Introduction

Since this is a book of studies that have been performed in the Netherlands, one may wonder whether the results presented here and the conclusions drawn will also be relevant for other countries. A direct answer to this question is, of course, not possible. The dilemmas we discuss here concern the choices individuals have to make in relation to their work and family life. Within Europe, countries vary as to what type of welfare state they represent and the degree of emancipation of women (Siaroff, 1995; Frinking & Willemsen, 1995). The context of these choices is also different. In the present chapter, I will describe the position of Dutch women and men in the international, mainly European, context. I will concentrate on the family situation and participation in the labour market, which are the two central areas of life to be discussed in this book.

Labour market participation of Dutch women

The participation of Dutch women in the labour market has changed rapidly, especially in the last two or three decades. After the second World War, girls normally ended their schooling at the age of 16. Only the rich ones went on to study or to receive some less formal education; most other girls went to work. However, as soon as they got married they generally stopped working. This was partly because of the general opinion that married women should not work; they should care for their husbands and later for their children. It was a husband's pride that his wife did not have to work, that he could earn enough money to sustain his wife or family. The trade unions strongly supported this male breadwinner model, and all kinds of tax laws gave breadwinners special benefits. This strong preference for the male breadwinner-cum-housewife model was also formalized in a law that forbid female civil servants and teachers from holding a paid job once they were married. This marriage law was only abolished in 1955.

Therefore, until the sixties we can describe the typical model woman's working career as having a job right out of school until marriage, a few years later, when she stopped working never to have a paid job again. We cannot really speak of a dilemma here, as the normalcy of the situation or even the legal impossibility of work after marriage in the case of civil servants, implied that women hardly had a choice at all. A woman had to have very strong feelings about her job to be able to keep on working after marriage and especially if she was also a mother. In that case, the dilemma was not between caring for her children or having a career, which is the main dilemma for women discussed in the present book, but between doing your vocation and doing what everybody, including your husband, wanted you to do. The main exceptions to this rule were the women who did not marry, the women with academic or other specific higher schooling, and women who were married to small-business men.

The latter form an interesting exception in the sense that here a different type of normalcy seems to operate. For shopkeepers, like grocery stores and other food shops, shoe and clothing shops, small cafes, it has always been completely normal that wife and husband work together, as it is too expensive to hire other personnel and most often the work is too much for one person. Officially, however, this was not considered working but helping out. If the wife fell ill she was not eligible for social security benefits. The same thing goes for farms. Here also, the work of the female farmer was not considered as such; it took the women's movement and then some twenty years, before women who were in charge of a large part of the work on their farm were considered farmers and not farmers' wives.

In the sixties, this pattern started to change, the main difference being that married women more often kept their jobs until the arrival of their first child. The years in between were often used to save enough money to be able to give the future children a good standard of living. This generation of women, who married in the sixties and seventies, often try to reenter the job market once the children are older. This turns out to be very difficult: only one in three women who wish to return to a paid job after having been jobless for 10 or more years succeeds in doing so (Vogels, 1995).

In the meantime two other processes have also changed. Women, and men, are becoming better educated. Since the beginning of the eighties, men and women in the Netherlands have had the same level of education. However, just as in the other European countries, so-called horizontal sex segregation still exists, i.e., women choose other majors, especially languages and the arts, whereas men more often choose technical studies. Another big change has been the postponement of the first pregnancy. In 1980, the age at which a woman first gave birth was 25.6 years, in 1995 this age was 28.6 years. This is the average; for certain groups of women, especially those with a higher education, the average age of giving birth to the first child is still about three years later. This average age is the highest worldwide. It shows that the dilemma between having a baby or having a career is one of the most pressing problems for women between the ages of 25 and 35 in the Netherlands, and its solution is often postponed.

Family status and paid work

In Table 1.1, an overview is given of the percentages of women and men who hold paid jobs in different age groups. We see from this table that in the youngest age group there is only a small difference between men and women; the younger ones are still at school, and the others have jobs. From the age of 25 on, the difference between women and men gets larger. Two effects are evident in this table. One is the cohort effect. As was explained before, women in the older age groups belong to the generation who stopped working after marriage or after the birth of their first child, resulting in low percentages of working women in that age group. The other effect is the child care effect, i.e., women in the 30-40 age range who have given up their jobs to take care of their children.

Table 1.1: Economic activity rate (% of the population who hold a job of at least 12 hours weekly or are officially registered as unemployed and actively looking for a job), of persons 15-64 years, in 1994

Age group	% Women	% Men
15-24	44	46
25-44	61	93
44-54	43	88
55-64	14	39
TOTAL	48	75

Source: Ministerie van Sociale Zaken en Werkgelegenheid (1995)

Table 1.2 specifies the latter effect. It shows how participation in the workforce of women, not men, is influenced by their family status. As long as there are no children married women have a paid job about as often as unmarried women. A single mother works far less often; more than half of them do not hold a paid job. Three out of four single fathers, however, have a paid job and probably hire child care. The biggest gender gap occurs in two-parent families with children under the age of 18. Here, by far, the largest percentage of men (94%) have a paid job, whereas the smallest percentage (45%) of women do. This is largely due to the fact that mothers leave the labour force once they have one or more children.

Not every mother quits her job after giving birth to her first child. Many mothers nowadays decide not to leave the working world at all, and keep on working, almost all of them in part-time jobs, as we will see in a moment. The most recent statistics show that only 41% of the mothers who have a job before their first child is born, stop working after the birth of their first child. Another 19% of those quit the workforce after their second child is born. The women who continue working most often reduce their working hours after a child is born.

Table 1.2: Economic activity rate (% of the population who hold a job of at least 12 hours weekly or are officially registered as unemployed and actively looking for a job) of women and men 15-64 years, according to their position in the household, in 1994

	% Women	% Men
One-person household	58	71
Household with partner, no children	46	75
One-parent family with child(ren) under 18	56	75
Two-parent family with child(ren) under 18	45	94
TOTAL	48	76

Source: Ministerie van Sociale Zaken en Werkgelegenheid (1995)

Table 1.3 shows the number of hours men and women work in various family situations. For men, we see that they more often work in full-time jobs once they have children. This 'reaction' to having children can be considered the traditional male way of taking care of your children by being a good provider. What is not visible in these figures is the new and still rare phenomenon of the new father, who, like his spouse/partner, works part-time and shares the responsibility for spending time on child care. These new patterns of fatherhood are discussed in Chapter 5; however, for a critical note on the phenomenon of the new father see Willemsen (1995).

Table 1.3: Hours of paid work per week, for women and men 15-64 years, according to their position in the household, in 1994

	% Women				% Men			
	No paid work	1-19 hrs	20-34 hrs	≥ 35 hrs	No paid work	1-19 hrs	20-34 hrs	≥ 35 hrs
One-person household	41	11	13	35	35	7	7	52
Household with partner, no children	58	9	20	28	36	-	-	57
One-parent family with child(ren) under 18	60	12	17	11	28	-	-	58
Two-parent family with child(ren) under 18	48	25	21	7	9	2	5	84
TOTAL	47	16	17	19	25	5	5	64

Source: Ministerie van Sociale Zaken en Werkgelegenheid (1995)

As is obvious from the figures in Tables 1.2 and 1.3, there are actually very few families with dependent children in which the fathers work part-time or are full-time househusbands. The typical pattern in the Netherlands is that women with children who have a partner either stop working or work part-time, whereas their partners work full-time.

The popularity of part-time work among women and its consequences

Dutch women - and men - more often work part-time than in any other country in Europe. This is illustrated in Table 1.4.

Table 1.4: Percentage of working people who work part-time, in 1992

Country	% Women	% Men
Belgium	28,1	2,1
Denmark	36,7	10,1
Germany	30,7	2,6
Greece	8,4	2,8
France	24,5	3,6
Ireland	18,6	3,9
Italy	11,5	2,9
Luxembourg	16,6	1,2
Netherlands	*63,8*	*15,4*
Portugal	11,3	4,1
Spain	13,7	2,0
United Kingdom	45,0	6,3

Source: Eurostat (1995)

Working part-time seems to be the favourite way to solve the children-career dilemma for women in the Netherlands (the relatively high percentage of part-time working men is mainly due to part-time early retirement). But how does this Dutch solution work out for women? Is part-time work the perfect solution to the child-career dilemma? That would be a very optimistic view of the situation. It turns out that having a small to moderate part-time job means full responsibility for household and child care tasks. This is illustrated by the figures in Table 1.5. Women who do not have a paid job spend a considerable amount of time on household and child care tasks; 44.5 hours, more than a normal work week. Their husbands also chip in almost 16 hours. At the other end of the range, women working full-time or almost full-time have cut back their household work considerably (other studies indicate that the hours of child care are not reduced; Groenendijk, 1994). These families often have hired help to assist them in reducing the load of household tasks. Moreover, the equality in hours of paid work coincides with an almost-equality in the unpaid work: men spend only slightly less time than women, 1.4 hours, on unpaid work, the smallest gender gap in unpaid work that has ever been seen in the Netherlands (and elsewhere, probably, but we do not have such detailed data available to test this assumption).

Table 1.5: Time used for household and care tasks by women and men, 20-64 years, cohabiting or married, specified according to women's paid work hours, in 1990

Women's paid work hours	Women	Men
Woman has no paid job	44,5	15,8
Woman works 1-9 hrs/week	41,2	13,3
Woman works 10-29 hrs/week	33,6	15,3
Woman works 30 or more hrs/week	18,5	17,1

Source: SCP (1994)

But what about the part-time working mothers, the large majority of working mothers? They spend considerably less time on household chores and child care than the full-time housewives, but, on the other hand, a lot more time than full-time working mothers. In fact, if we add the hours for paid and unpaid work, we see that the part-time working mothers have the largest task load of all groups. These women form the embodiment of the 'double burden.' Their spouses, however, do not do very much to help them out; they put in even less hours than the spouses of full-time housewives! The data in Table 1.5 are from 1990. For 1995, the available time budget data for the Netherlands have not yet been analyzed in a comparable way. However, it is clear that the trend for men to spend more time on household and child care tasks has continued. On the other hand, men who work more than 20 hours a week in a paid job still have more leisure time, that is, time without work or care obligations, than women in a comparable situation: 40.6 hours compared to 37.3 hours. In fact, women who work (nearly) full-time have the fewest hours of leisure of all the groups studied in the survey (SCP, 1996).

In the chapter by Van der Vinne and Brink, the psychological background of this situation, especially how spouses cope with the seeming injustice of the double burden, is discussed in more detail. On a general level, one can easily understand why part-time work is a trap. The reason that women choose to work part-time is generally because that gives them more time to take care of their children and the household. By giving this reason, both to others and to themselves, they voluntarily agree that the housework and child care are their responsibilities, that they are the ones who have time for these tasks. Their spouses are thus legitimized in thinking that they, with their full-time jobs, don't have to do any household chores. This seems rather logical. People don't count hours of housework and child care, as researchers do. Only paid work is measured in that way. Therefore the overburdening of women in terms of the combination of paid and unpaid work is a typical researchers' problem, not even always recognized by the women it concerns. Nevertheless, it is legitimate to call it a problem since, for instance, the medical effects of this work load are becoming apparent. In a recent large study of tiredness it turned out that particularly mothers and managers suffer from chronic fatigue (Bensing & Schreurs, 1995).

Circumstances are such that this situation will probably not change in the near future. The available child care in the Netherlands for children under the age of 4 is very limited. There are different forms of day care, but the one that is most useful for working parents, where a child can be looked after for entire days, is only available for 4% of children under the age of 4. Kindergarten starts at 4 for all children. That does not mean that from that age on parents have fewer worries about child care; on the contrary, school days are short and many schools still have long midday breaks when children are supposed to go home for lunch, although provisions for staying at school are now a legal obligation for all schools.

The Netherlands compared to other countries

We have seen that the Netherlands has the largest proportion of part-time work of all countries in Europe. A well-recognized side-effect of part-time work is that it keeps women in jobs that are not as well-paid as full-time jobs; at least, that is the explanation offered by the official institutes for the gender gap in average hourly wages. But it is not only with respect to earnings that a gender gap occurs.

In 1995, the Human Development Report published annually by the United Nations, paid special attention to gender differences. As usual, this report contains the Human Development Index (HDI), an index based on indicators for longevity, educational attainment, and standard of living, for many nations in the world. In 1995, the report also contained the Gender-related Development Index (GDI), based on the same variables as the HDI but adjusted for the degree of disparity in achievement between men and women. The Netherlands scored very high on the general HDI, coming in fourth, preceded only by Canada, the United States, and Japan. On the GDI, however, the ranking was dramatically lower: the Netherlands ranked 20th. The main reason for this drop in ranking is the fact

that women's share of the total earned income is only 25.2 %. Table 1.6 shows the HDI
and GDI for a selection of countries. Compared to European countries and the previously
mentioned three industrial countries ahead of the Netherlands in general development, the
Netherlands has the one but biggest gender gap. Only Spain has a larger difference between
the absolute values and the ranks of the two indices.

*Table 1.6: Human Development Index (HDI) and Gender-related Development Index
(GDI) for a selection of countries, mainly EU*

Country	HDI	GDI	GDI-rank *	HDI-rank minus GDI rank
Canada	0.950	0.891	9	- 8
USA	0.937	0.901	5	- 3
Japan	0.937	0.896	8	- 5
Netherlands	0.936	0.851	20	-16
Finland	0.934	0.918	2	3
France	0.930	0.898	7	0
Spain	0.930	0.795	34	-26
Sweden	0.929	0.919	1	8
Belgium	0.926	0.852	18	- 7
Austria	0.925	0.882	10	3
Denmark	0.920	0.904	4	10
UK	0.916	0.862	13	3
Ireland	0.915	0.813	30	-13
Italy	0.912	0.861	14	4
Greece	0.907	0.825	27	- 8
Portugal	0.874	0.832	25	5

*) rank in a world-wide list of 130 countries

Source: United Nations Development Programme (1995)

Attitudes

The shortage of child care and the large gender gap in paid work and other aspects contrast sharply with the very progressive attitudes of the Dutch with regards to sex roles, child education, and similar matters. We will first compare attitudes on a general level with those from a few other countries. For such a comparison, data are available from the Attitude Towards Women Scale (AWS; Spence and Helmreich, 1972), an often used reliable and valid instrument to assess attitudes toward sex roles. Although it's name suggests that attitudes towards women are measured, the scale actually consists of items that pertain to areas such as equal responsibility of spouses in matters of education of the children, acceptability of mothers having a career, and similar sex role aspects. Morinaga, Frieze and Ferligoj (1993) performed an international study comparing the AWS scores of students in three countries: the United States, Japan, and Slovenia. For the United States, data from a general adult sample are available from Nelson (1988). I used the scale in the Netherlands both in studies with student samples (Willemsen, 1992) and in a survey with random sample of adults (20-70 years) (Willemsen, 1995, unpublished data). As is apparent from Table 1.7, the Dutch respondents are far more progressive than the corresponding groups of other subjects. In general, in each country, women score more progressively on this scale than

Table 1.7: Mean item scores [1] on the Attitudes Towards Women Scale for samples from different countries

	Women	Men
student samples		
U.S. [2]	4.01	3.65
Japan [2]	3.62	3.29
Slovenia [2]	4.08	3.81
Netherlands [3]	4.41	4.10
adult samples		
U.S. [4]	3.82	3.50
Netherlands [5]	4.08	3.86

[1] 1 = very traditional   5 = very progressive
[2] Data from Morinaga et al. (1993)
[3] Data from Willemsen (1992)
[4] Data from Nelson (1988)
[5] Unpublished data from Willemsen (1995)

men; the gender gap is, on average, about 0.3 on a 5-point scale. In the Netherlands, we see the same gender differences, in the student sample as well as in the adult sample. Dutch men, however, are more progressive than women in most other countries.

The large national opinion polls that are held every few years show that the opinions on the desirability of mothers who work have changed drastically over the last decades. In 1965, 84% of the Dutch population found it objectionable if a married woman with children worked. In 1995, this proportion of persons with objections shrunk to only 16% of the population. If, however, working implies that children have to go to a child care centre the percentage of people who object is a lot higher. In 1995, 39% were still opposed (SCP, 1996). Although the attitudes of both men and women are rather egalitarian, it seems one is not quite willing to accept the consequences of such an attitude, at least not if it means that both husband and wife spend a lot of time at work and part of the child care has to be performed by professionals.

If we ask young men and women how they would solve these dilemmas we get a moderately egalitarian answer. In a survey by the Equal Opportunity Board of Amsterdam University (1993), male and female students were asked how they envisaged their future in this respect. Of the female students, 56% predicted they would have a part-time job between the ages of 30 and 40, whereas 35% of the male students predicted the same for themselves, i.e., expected to be working part-time between the ages of 30 and 40. Obviously, as a comparison with the figures in Tables 1.2 and 1.3 shows, the women's prediction is much more realistic than the men's.

From these and other studies we get the impression that Dutch men have good intentions toward egalitarianism and solidarity, and that they envisage leading a more egalitarian life than their parents. However, at the critical moment, which, in the Netherlands occurs after the birth of their first child, men do not realize these intentions but overwhelmingly choose for the traditional provider role. At the moment, this traditional role behaviour of men seems to be the consequence of their spouses' choice for motherhood (Willemsen, 1994).

Conclusion

Dutch men and women are quite progressive, both in terms of general attitudes towards sex roles and in terms of a certain tolerance for working mothers. They do not seem too attached to the traditional role patterns. However, as soon as the situation arises where a decision on task division is needed, i.e., after the birth of the first child, men do not, in fact, cut back to part-time work, with few exceptions. Some men work even more hours so that the average work week of young fathers is longer than that of men without children. Young mothers often work part-time and, at the same time, have responsibility for the household and for child care. The awareness that their husbands intended to work part-time and take part in the housework and care of the children will be small comfort to them.

As is the case in many other fields of study, with respect to family life, opinions and attitudes change faster than actual behaviours. However, we have come a long way since the fifties. The situation where a woman, once married, stops working never to resume paid work again, is far behind us. Whatever the reasons, the discrepancy between attitudes and opinions, and behaviour makes the Netherlands an appropriate place for the study of dilemmas. Because this attitude-behaviour gap is so large, it is expected that the dilemmas are more complex in the Netherlands than elsewhere. There is a public awareness that opinions and behaviours are inconsistent, and many institutions try to invent strategies to make the daily life of men and women more in accordance with their expressed opinions. At the state and organizational levels, as well as on an individual level, many people are doing their best to bridge this gap. In the last chapter of this book more attention will be paid to these policies.

Although the gap between attitudes and behaviours may be large in the Netherlands, this discrepancy represents a type of problem women and men encounter in modern life all over the Western world. In every Western country men earn more money than women and women do more household and child care tasks than men (Eurostat, 1995; UNDP, 1995). However, women put in more hours of paid work than they used to, a development that is encouraged and supported by policy measures in most countries, especially in Europe (Willemsen & Frinking, 1995). Therefore, it is to be expected that, in the Netherlands as elsewhere, men and women will experience many dilemmas, at certain times in their lives, between the attraction of paid work and the advantages of the traditional solution of the full-time-breadwinner-with-full-time-housewife situation. The most important ones will be discussed in the remaining chapters, from a macro point of view, as well as from the standpoint of women, men, and couples.

References

Bensing, J.M. & K. Schreurs (1995). Sekseverschillen bij moeheid [Sex differences in tiredness]. *Huisarts en Wetenschap, 33*, 412-421.

Emancipatiecommissie Vrouwen aan de UvA [Equal Opportunity Board Amsterdam University] (1993). *Resultaten van de studentenenquête ter gelegenheid van 8 maart 1993* [Results of the survey among students for the occasion of March 8th, 1993]. Amsterdam University, unpublished report.

Eurostat (1995). *Women and men in the European Union.* Luxembourg: Office for Official Publications of the European Communities.

Frinking, G.A.B. & T.M. Willemsen (1995). Introduction: Policies regarding the gender division of paid and unpaid work in Europe. In T.M. Willemsen & G.A.B. Frinking (Eds.), *Work and family in Europe: The role of policies* (pp. 1-6). Tilburg: Tilburg University Press.

Groenendijk, H. (1994). Werken is zorgen: een tegenstelling voorbij [To work is to care: beyond a contradiction]. *Tijdschrift voor Vrouwenstudies, 15*, 525-532.

Ministerie van Sociale Zaken en Werkgelegenheid (1995). *Emancipatie in cijfers 1995*. Den Haag: Ministerie SZW.

Morinaga, Y., I.H. Frieze & A. Ferligoj (1993). Career plans and gender-role attitudes of college students in the United States, Japan, and Slovenia. *Sex Roles, 29*, 317-334.

Nelson, M.C. (1988). Reliability, validity and cross-cultural comparisons for the simplified Attitudes Toward Women Scale. *Sex Roles, 18*, 289-296.

Siaroff, A. (1995). Work, welfare and gender equality. In D. Sainsbury (Ed.), *Gendering welfare states*, pp. 82-101. London: Sage.

Sociaal en Cultureel Planbureau (SCP) (1994). *Sociaal Cultureel Rapport 1994*. Rijswijk: SCP.

Sociaal en Cultureel Planbureau (SCP) (1996). *Sociaal Cultureel Rapport 1996*. Rijswijk: SCP.

Spence, J. T. & R.L. Helmreich (1972). The Attitudes towards Women Scale: An objective instrument to measure attitudes toward the rights and roles of women in contemporary society. *Catalog of Selected Documents in Psychology, 2*, 66.

United Nations Development Programme (UNDP) (1995). *Human Development Report 1995*. Oxford: Oxford University Press.

Vogels, R. (1995). *Continuïteit en discontinuïteit in de loopbanen van vrouwen* [Continuity and discontinuity in women's careers]. Tilburg: Tilburg University Press.

Willemsen, T.M. (1992). Sekse als cognitieve categorie [Gender as a cognitive category]. In T. Top & J. Heesink (Eds.), *Psychologie en sekse* [Psychology and gender]. Houten: Bohn Stafleu van Loghum.

Willemsen, T.M. (1994). Aan goede bedoelingen geen gebrek. Over individualisme en solidariteit in huwelijksrelaties. [No lack of good intentions. Individualism and solidarity in marriage]. In A. van den Broek & B. Seuren (Eds), *Individualisme en solidariteit* [Individualism and solidarity], pp. 35-46. Tilburg: Tilburg University Press.

Willemsen, T.M. (1995). From typologies to diversities. A note on studying 'new fathers'. In M.C.P. van Dongen, G.A.B. Frinking & M.J.G. Jacobs (Eds.), *Changing fatherhood. An interdisciplinary perspective*. Amsterdam: Thesis.

Willemsen, T.M. & G.A.B. Frinking (Eds.) (1995). *Work and family in Europe: The role of policies*. Tilburg: Tilburg University Press.

2

Women between motherhood and employment:
A historical overview from different perspectives

Ad Vossen
Jan Nelissen

Introduction

One of the main issues of modern social policy is whether or not to support women by removing the existing incompatibilities between motherhood and employment, in other words whether or not to contribute to solve a classic dilemma situation. The useful effect of policy measures depends, to a great extent, on reliable and accurate knowledge of the dynamic and complex interrelationship between having children and a holding paid job. With this article we hope to make a contribution to the field and have chosen for a descriptive, macro approach. In order to get a more detailed view, employment and motherhood will be studied from different time perspectives.

In the early 1960's, the fertility level of the Netherlands nearly topped the European list. Only Albania and Ireland had higher figures. However, in a period of only 10 years, from 1965 to 1975, the average number of children per woman dropped from 3.1 to 1.6 and has more or less stabilized. This unparalleled and dramatic fall in fertility makes Dutch demographic history unique. At the beginning of the 'second demographic transition' (Van der Kaa, 1987), more than 40% of all births were third or fourth children: 10 years later the share of these higher parities had fallen to only 16% (Beets, 1993).

The end of the drastic fertility decrease in 1975 coincided with the beginning of a period in which the labour force participation of women began a substantial rise. From an international point of view, the Netherlands has always lagged behind in female labour participation and is only recently catching up (WRR, 1990; OECD, 1991). The strong growth of female employment since 1975 is mainly due to a massive entry of married women into the workforce, usually working in part-time functions (Mertens, Schippers & Siegers, 1992). This explains that, in spite of the fact that about 56% of Dutch adult women have a paid job nowadays, only 30% of all paid work is done by women (SCP, 1993). In this respect there is a remarkable discrepancy in the Netherlands between relatively positive attitudes towards working mothers - or more generally, towards egalitarian gender roles - and the relatively low actual employment rate of married women (Haller & Hoellinger, 1994). Recent opinion surveys show that only about 16% of the Dutch population opposes the combination of motherhood and employment, while this figure was as high as 84% in 1965 (SCP, 1996).

A lot of effort has been made to explain the late entry of Dutch women into the workforce (Pott-Buter, 1993; Mertens, Van Doorne-Huiskes, Schippers & Siegers, 1995). Some researchers feel the main cause is a very persistent motherhood ideology, strongly supported by the Church, which does not allow mothers to leave the care of their children to other people. Others, especially (socio-)economists, refer to late industrialization, high male salaries, and social security arrangements and fiscal regulations that have always favoured families with a mother at home. The recent growth in labour participation by married women may be a result of higher levels of education and the growing number of part-time jobs.

The research tradition in the field of the competitive character of fertility and labour participation is relatively long and extensive. For detailed reviews and evaluations we refer the reader to Spitze (1988), Siegers, De Jong-Gierveld & Van Imhoff (1991), and Bernhardt (1993). The most prominent theoretical point of interest has always been the causal relationship between motherhood and employment. Research findings have been far from univocal in this respect (e.g., Klijzing, Siegers, Keilman & Groot, 1988). When looking for the largest common denominator, the results may be summarized as follows: there is a substantive negative influence of the presence of children on labour participation, and a less pronounced or even absent negative causal flow from labour participation towards fertility.

When roughly classifying these studies, a distinction can be made between *micro* approaches, usually aimed at explaining the mutual causal effect of motherhood and employment from different theoretical frameworks (in which rational choice theory dominates), and *macro* approaches, generally more restricted in their pretentions, and describing and interpreting the relationship at stake at a higher level of aggregation, thus looking for historical patterns of change and differences between populations. In addition to these differences in aggregation level, studies in the field of the interrelationship between family formation and employment can be characterized by the time dimension chosen. As such, processes of change can be established from a cross-sectional (*transversal*) angle, or from a cohort-succession (*longitudinal*) point of view. The rationale behind the longitudinal study of processes of social change was introduced in demography by Whelpton (1949), while Ryder made a significant contribution to this discussion in his classical article 'The cohort as a concept in the study of social change' (Ryder, 1965). Since then, numerous theoretical and empirical studies have elaborated on this theme (Ryder, 1980; Becker, 1992) and have illustrated that 'social change can be better understood by looking at the life histories of successive generations and cohorts' (Blossfeld, 1992, p. 97). The underlying logic of cohort analysis has been clearly expressed by Lindenberg: 'Thus, cohorts are indelibly marked by their particular socialization throughout their existence in the system. This mark will show up even though it might be pushed around a bit by period effects (i.e. events that affect all cohorts) and life cycle effects (i.e. events that typically affect people in a particular phase of their life cycle)' (Lindenberg, 1992, p. 284). Taking this for granted - and considering motherhood and female employment behaviour as indicators of social change - we can hypothize that patterns of demographic reproduction, as well as patterns of female employment as studied from a cohort's perspective, should yield more insight into its true historical course than comparable patterns based on transversal observations. Although methodologists have developed formal techniques (*A*(ge)-*P*(eriod)-*C*(ohort)-models) for reducing historical changes into these different kinds of effects (Mason & Fienberg, 1985; Hagenaars, 1990), this chapter will be restricted to a more tentative, less formalized type of analysis.

After introducing the operationalization of the main concepts and the microsimulation data used, motherhood and employment profiles will be presented from both a cohort succession and a cross-sectional time dimension.

Operationalization of the main concepts

The aforementioned studies often differ in the way they operationalize the key concepts under study, which is due to specific research questions and the availability of data.

Earlier research has repeatedly pointed to the fact that the *presence* of young children in the household, an indicator of the motherhood concept, has proved to be one of the most important determinants of female labour force participation. According to Jones (1982), presence of children should be composed, in this respect, of two factors. The first is the direct impact of a birth, initially quite negative, and the second is the declining probability of working outside the home as the number of children grows. The present analysis combines these two components into the concept of 'motherhood career.' This variable has been operationalized in *motherhood profiles*, consisting of a series of age-specific proportions of women with the youngest child in the household in the age group 0-17. Within this crude age grouping, a specification has been made into subgroups (0-5, 6-11, and 12-17 years). The use of profiles has the advantage that a clear distinction can be made between quantities representing the intensity of the phenomenon and quantities measuring timing or localization aspects. Within birth cohorts, the quantity measuring the intensity aspect of the motherhood profile can be described as *the average number of years spent in a birth cohort as the 'mother of a younger child'* (C.MY). Its transversal equivalent, P.MY, constructed on calender year-based observations - or synthetic cohorts as they are sometimes called - has basically the same meaning. Synthetic cohorts, however, are heterogeneous units of analysis in the sense that they are composed of a cross-section of real cohorts, each with its own background and exposure to main historical events (wars, economic depressions). From an analytical point of view the aggregate intensity quantity MY is rather hybrid in character.[1]

The intensity variable MY is, as a construct, comparable to the demographic quantity 'life expectancy,' though the former is a crude measure that does not correct for mortality and migration. Since, however, the impact of both variables is only marginal and occurs in all (synthetic) cohorts, the validity of this quantity is not seriously jeopardized.

The timing factor included in the motherhood profile will be expressed as the quantity AM: *the average age of a mother of a younger child.* In the case of cohorts, C.AM will be used, while the average age in periods will be indicated as P.AM. The constituting elements of MY and AM are generated by microsimulation.

The data produced by the microsimulation model NEDYMAS (see next section), also offer a unique opportunity for a longitudinal and transversal analysis of female employment careers over a substantial period of time, and are not hampered by changing definitions and other practical problems. Besides, since the data are differentiated with respect to part-time/full-time factors, they enable us to determine employment in terms of *persons* as well as *person-years*. Analogous to the analysis of motherhood profiles, employment profiles can be characterized by a volume quantity and a timing quantity. The former has been expressed as a variable named EY (or, specified according to the time perspective, C.EY for cohort observations and P.EY for period observations), measuring the *average number of years in a (synthetic) cohort that women are employed in a paid job.*[2] When analyzing employment profiles in terms of person-years, the variable EPY (or C.EPY and P.EPY) will be used, to indicate the average length of participation in person-years.

To elucidate the meaning of the variables used to operationalize the concepts 'motherhood' and 'employment profiles,' we present their values for the cohort grouping 1930-1932.

$C.MY_{30\text{-}32}$ =   *15.0 years*, meaning that in the 1930-1932 cohorts women were, within their total life span, mother of a child under 18 for an average of 15.0 years.

$C.AM_{30\text{-}32}$ =   *38.4 years*, indicating the average age of a mother of a child under 18.

$C.EY_{30\text{-}32}$ =   *15.9 years*, meaning that, on average, women in this cohort grouping had a paid job for 15.9 years of their life span, regardless of the number of working hours per week.

$C.EPY_{30\text{-}32}$=   *12.1 years*, meaning that, in terms of person-years, on average 12.1 years were spent working full-time.

---

[1]   As such, MY reflects not only the average number of children brought forth by a (synthetic) cohort (or, more specifically, a series of parity progression rates), but also the length of birth intervals. The timing aspect (the mean age of the mother of a younger child: AM, see below) contains effects of the mother's age at the birth of her first and last child.

[2]   Like the variable MY, EY is a gross quantity in the sense that it has not been corrected for the demographic factors.

Referring to discussions in the introduction regarding the choice between a longitudinal and a transversal time perspective, we formulate the following, more specific, expectations.

(1) As far as the parameters of the motherhood profile are concerned, a longitudinal analysis should show, at the intra-cohort level, more *regularity* in the shape of the overall profile (MY_{0-17}) than a transversal analysis, since the parameters of the former are, at least theoretically, less disturbed by periodical effects than the parameters of the latter. Actual cohorts should yield a stronger *consistency* in the relationship between the partial MY's (MY_{0-5}, MY_{6-11} and MY_{12-17}) than synthetic cohorts. It is reasonable that these parameters should show decreasing values. Since parities vary (some women will have only one child, others two or more) within (synthetic) cohorts, the total years spent being a mother of a youngest child 0-5 years old, should exceed the number of years spent as a mother of a youngest child between 6 and 11 years, and so on.

(2) The second expectation deals with the inter-cohort developments over time, and is based on empirical demographic evidence. Historical analysis of fertility in the Netherlands shows a steady, regular decline in total cohort fertility rates (CFR) from the beginning of the last decade in the 19th century up to now. The course of its transversal equivalent (TFR), however, is considerably less regular and is, in fact, dominated by a prolonged period (1945-1965) of high birth rates, followed by a steep decline (1965-1975). For the most part the 'birth plateau' phenomenon can be explained by a sharp, structural transition process in the timing of births that took place within cohorts. A tendency to marry at a younger age, in combination with short birth intervals, has been quickly followed by the opposite trend of a sharp increase in the age at which women give birth to their first child (Janssen & Vossen, 1986). Given the fact that our fertility parameter MY and the traditional total fertility rates, CFR and TFR, are both indicators of the same fertility regime, we expect a more regular development in the cohort's MY (C.MY) than in the period's MY (P.MY). At the same time, the transitional movement in the longitudinal timing pattern, as described above, has to be traced in the course of the localization parameter AM.

The Data

Microsimulation is a 'technique of computerized modelling within which the decision-making process is replicated for individual decision-makers within the system' (Bonsall, 1979, p. 82). In short, microsimulation looks at certain aspects of the life course of individuals, applying transition rates based on empirical observations.

Microsimulation data is used for two reasons. In the first place, existing demographic and (socio-)economic data do not allow us to appropriately describe motherhood or employment careers from a longitudinal perspective. Secondly, definitions of labour participation have changed frequently in the period under study making it hard to standardize existing statistics satisfactorily. Figure 2.A.1.1 (see Appendix A) depicts the time dimension of the analyses. Since simulation starts in 1947, the 1930 birth cohort is the first one whose motherhood and employment career can be followed completely. Observations were used up to 1990; and subsequently (official) forecasts were used. In other words, the profiles of the oldest cohorts are almost completely based on observations, while those of the youngest cohorts are mostly based on projections. The transversal or cross-sectional analyses cover the period from 1960-1995. Data for the last 5-year interval have been derived from authorized economic and demographic forecasts. In order to have a more solid basis, the longitudinal as well as the transversal data were aggregated in grouped observation units of 3 years. The time frame was chosen in such a way that the interval between the first cohort (1930-32) and the first period (1960-62) is 30 years, a value approximating one generation (Vossen & Nelissen, 1994).

The data used for the present analyses were produced by the dynamic, cross-sectional microsimulation model NEDYMAS.[3] In this specific case, microsimulation created a synthetic database reflecting developments in the demographic and economic structure of the population. The dynamic approach implies that demographic processes are explicitly simulated, which means that the size of the microdata base changes during the simulation period. The sample passed through time, year by year. For each individual in the microdata base it was determined which personal characteristics change each year, and to what extent. An overview of the ins and outs of the microsimulation approach can be found in Citro & Hanushek (1991).

NEDYMAS is based on three interrelated modules: a demographic module, a labour market and income formation module, and a social security module. More detailed information on the characteristics of this microsimulation model is given in Appendix A.

Motherhood profiles

In this section a description will be given of the motherhood profiles as defined above, and we will determine whether the results concerning the differences between the longitudinal and transversal data meet our expectations as stated at the end of the second section. In separate subsections, cohort observations and period observations will be evaluated.

---

[3]   NEDYMAS stands for *NE*therlands *DY*namic *M*icro-*A*nalytic *S*imulation model; see Nelissen (1994).

Cohort observations

Figure 2.B.1 (Appendix B) depicts some of the microsimulation results. For a selection of the birth cohorts under study, it shows the overall profile as well as subprofiles for specific age groups of young children.

In viewing the overall profiles we find that, in accordance with our expectations, their shape is very regular indeed and that the C.MY values closely follow a normal distribution. At the same time, however, a strict trend-like change over time at the inter-cohort level is not evident. There is no steady decline, for instance, in the highest C.MY values (the top of the curve), nor in the development of the variance of the distributions. This kind of irregularity is partly reflected in the total volume or intensity parameter and the average number of years spent as mother of a youngest child under 18. The historical inter-cohort pattern is shown in Figure 2.1.1. It can be seen from this figure that women in the 1930-1932 birth cohort had to take care of a younger child for an average of 15 years. For the most recent cohort (1963-1965) that figure drops to approximately 11 years. Cohorts in the centre of the period described (1942-1944 up to and including 1948-1950) show some deviations from the general descending trend. In general, the same irregularities are observed in the cohorts' CFR (Cohort Fertility Rate), a volume quantity that is not influenced by changing timing patterns and birth intervals (Janssen & Vossen, 1986). In looking at Figure 2.1.2, which shows the average age of mothers with a younger child (C.AM), we see that the irregularities in the cohort's MY coincide with the structural trend disturbance in the C.AM values. It is therefore plausible that the sudden changes in the timing pattern of births have affected these C.MY and CFR values.

If we examine the subprofiles (Figure 2.B.1) by breaking down the overall profile into three equal age categories (0-5; 6-11; 12-17) of the youngest child, we find that the intra-cohort relationship between the subprofiles in all cases meets the consistency requirements (see second section). Within each cohort every subsequent profile exceeds the preceding one. The largest difference is found for the volume of $C.MY_{0-5}$ on the one hand and the volume of both $C.MY_{6-11}$ and $C.MY_{12-17}$ on the other. As C.MY is a hybrid quantity, the differences between the subprofiles are the mixed result of the parity progression pattern of a cohort and the differences in the duration of birth intervals. The figures show that, over time, not only do all partial C.MY's decrease but the difference between $C.MY_{0-5}$ and the other age-specific C.MY's is also diminishing. This is partly due to the fact that higher parities are becoming more scarce, and that the variance in the final number of children within a cohort decreases.

Finally, Figure 2.1.2, shows the longitudinal trajectory of the timing variable C.AM. For every age group we see a decline (in mean age at which women have their youngest child) until cohort 1945-1947, followed by an almost constant upswing. This movement can be considered an exponent of the more obvious tendency of women to postpone motherhood.

Figure 2.1: Motherhood: cohort versus period observations

2.1.1 C.MY cohort observations

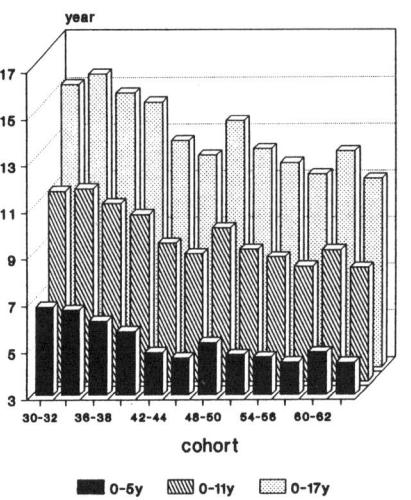

2.1.2 C.AM cohort observations

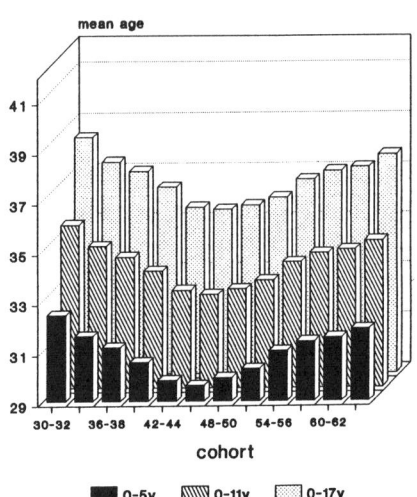

2.1.3 P.MY period observations

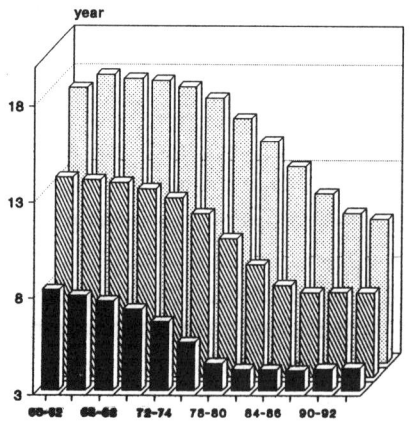

2.1.4 P.AM period observations

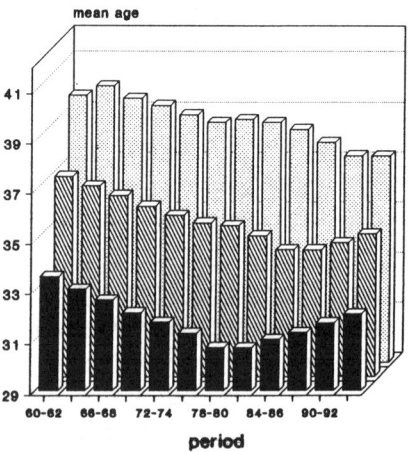

This interpretation is in accordance with conclusions from earlier analyses based on vital statistics (Janssen & Vossen, 1986).

Period observations

After reviewing the longitudinal motherhood data we will now look for similarities and differences that result from a transversal ordering of the same simulation results. It should be noted that the overlap between the two data sets is not complete (see Figure 2.A.1.1). In contrast to the cohort observations which were partly based on official forecast results, period observations largely stem from factual input data. As mentioned in the data section, cohorts and periods were chosen such that the difference between the first period observations (1960-1962) and the first cohort observations (1930-1932) amounts to 30 years, the approximate value of a generation, which is conventionally used as a criterion in demographic translation techniques to provide a basis for comparison between cohorts and periods.

Figure 2.B.2 (Appendix B) shows a selection of the motherhood profiles while an overall picture of cross-sectional P.MY and P.AM values is presented in Figures 2.1.3 and 2.1.4. It is obvious from the shape of the profiles that they are less regular than their longitudinal counterparts, and deviate sharply from a normal distribution. These irregularities are, for the most part, the consequence of the structural changes in C.AM for cohorts (a gradual decline followed by a sudden upswing) that was observed in the longitudinal analysis. So, we are dealing here with typical cohort effects. The longitudinal counterparts of the period 1960-1974 are the 1930-1944 cohorts that witnessed decreasing C.AM values. The turning point in the latter was observed in the 1948-1950 cohort, and is, according to our translation scheme, on average reflected in the 1978-1980 period data. The following increase in cohort C.AM is expressed in the irregularities manifested in the shape of the period observations between 1980 and 1995. The distribution of the most recent period, 1993-1995, slowly regains a normal form, highlighting the fact that the impact of the structural transition of the timing pattern is gradually fading out and a more or less stable situation might be established. As far as the subprofiles are concerned, we clearly see that, contrary to the longitudinal data, they do not meet the intra-cohort consistency criterion introduced earlier. In particular, after the turning point in P.AM has been reached, there are periods in which P.MY's of higher age categories exceed those of lower age categories, which is, in fact, highly illogical.

Figure 2.1.3 depicts an overall view of the development of P.MY for the period under study. Compared to the cohort observations, the historical pattern is now obviously smoother. After a slow decline in the first part of the period, an acceleration took place between 1969-1971 and 1981-1983 (for the youngest age group), followed by a more stabilized course. Within this period P.MY decreased from 18 years to about 10.5 years

(41%). This decline in years spent as a mother of a younger child is more dramatic than the decline witnessed by cohorts, as described in the previous subsection. A robust change in the timing pattern emerging in cohorts, is intensified in P.MY period observations. As far as AM (the mean age of the mother of a younger child) is concerned, transversal data show a less pronounced trend rupture, compared to longitudinal data (Figure 2.1.4). This can be explained by the fact that cross-sectional observations are the result of a mixture of cohorts, some of which reproduce themselves according to 'pre-transitional' patterns, while more recent cohorts conform to 'post'-transitional patterns.

Motherhood profiles: a review
Let us now briefly review the main results of the analyses and compare them with the ex ante expectations as stated at the end of the second section.

Our first prediction was that a longitudinal description would yield more regular and consistent profiles at the *intra-cohort/intra-period* level, since ' ... cohorts are indelibly marked by their particular socialization throughout their existence in the system' (Lindenberg, 1992, p. 284). Although the latter were, of course, also exposed to period effects, they were expected to be dominated by specific cohort effects. As we have seen before, this proposition was confirmed. The shape of the cohort profiles is much more regular than the period profiles, and the cohorts' subprofiles do meet the consistency criterion, contrary to the periods subprofiles.

Furthermore it was assumed that the longitudinal trajectory in C.MY values would show a gradual and steady decline at the *inter-cohort/inter-period* level, whereas the transversal trajectory was expected to be affected by typical period effects. Comparing Figures 2.1.1 and 2.1.3 however, shows that P.MY runs more smoothly if we consider period data. As mentioned in the previous subsections, the temporary disturbance of C.MY witnessed by the 1942-1950 cohorts can be explained by a historically unique and 'explosive' transition of the timing pattern, a phenomenon in which magnitude is suppressed in the transversal or cross-sectional time perspective, due to the presence of a mixture of cohorts at different stages in the transition process.

Employment profiles

As noted above, data generated by NEDYMAS enables both longitudinal and transversal analyses of female employment careers, as they are unhindered by definition problems and other practical problems, like transforming non-continuous, cross-sectional data into continuous longitudinal data. Since the data are differentiated with respect to the number of hours worked per week, it is possible to measure employment in terms of *persons* as well as *person-years*. In addition to full-time employment (≥ 32 hours per week), two categories of part-time employment are distinguished (1-19 hours and 20-31 hours per week). Employment profiles consist of a series of age-specific participation rates, calculated for a specific cohort or period. Analogous to the analysis of motherhood profiles, employment profiles can be characterized by a volume (or intensity) quantity, and by a timing (or localization) quantity. The intensity quantity has been expressed in a variable, EY, which stands for the average number of years in a (synthetic) cohort's life span that women have been employed in a paid job (either full-time or part-time). Like the variable MY, introduced in the previous section, EY is a gross quantity in the sense that it has not been adjusted for the demographic factors mortality and migration. When analyzing employment profiles in terms of person-years, the variable EPY was used, indicating the average length of participation expressed in person-years. The description of timing characteristics of the profile were omitted, because, in contrast to the motherhood profile, employment patterns do not show the kind of regularity that enables them to be parameterized.

Cohort observations
Figure 2.B.3 (see Appendix B) contains a series of graphs, describing (a selection of) the employment profiles *in persons* for the 1930-1932 to 1963-1965 cohorts. In each of these graphs, four profiles are presented. The upper line depicts the profile of total, or overall, participation rates (sum of part-time plus full-time employment).

Generally speaking, the shape of the employment profile is quite different from that of the motherhood profile, which comes very near to a normal distribution. The first graph in Figure 2.B.3 (1930-1932 cohort), shows the typical structure of the traditional employment profile: a bi-modal distribution that peaks at post-school ages (with a participation rate of 62% at age 20-22). This peak is followed by a long, steep fall (mainly due to motherhood) to a level of well over 20%, which, after the age of 40, gradually leads to a second peak with a participation rate of 35% in the early 50s. Another decrease follows, caused by early retirement, which completes the profile.[4] The same graph also shows that up to the age of 40, nearly all women with a paid job were employed full-time. Subsequently, the number of part-timers increased. This category consists of women who changed from a full-time to a part-time job, as well as mothers of older children (re-)entering the labour market. Assuming that women with full-time jobs within the 25-44 age group (about 20% of the entire female population) are mainly unmarried or married but childless, the extremely low part-time employment rates indicate that very few women in this early cohort had parallel careers.

The series of graphs give us an overview of the changes that took (or will take) place

---

[4]   For the cohorts born between 1933 and 1962, the very last age group showed a slight recovery, probably due to the fact that full-time jobs were split up into part-time jobs.

between the oldest cohort, 1930-1932, and the recent cohort, 1960-1962, which is composed of actual observations for women under 30, while participation of the higher age groups is based on forecasts.

Figure 2.2.1 sketches the differences for total employment between four selected cohorts. It shows that the profile's original and pronounced bi-modal structure has undergone, and will undergo, drastic changes. As a result of prolonged education and postponed motherhood, the original top of the employment profile decreases by about 12 percentage points, and gradually shifts to the next higher age group. The profile as a whole gets somewhat flatter, though its volume (intensity) grows sharply. The typical 'children gap' (low participation rates in the period when women have younger children) becomes less articulated. The two most recent cohorts show a substantive increase in participation rates at relatively high ages (50 and over). This is mainly based on assumptions presented in recent Dutch labour supply forecasts (increasing educational level within cohorts; smaller families and a growing proportion of childless women; labour market shortages after the year 2000, due to population ageing).

The intensity value, C.EY (the surface under the overall profile), will increase from 15.9 years for the oldest cohort to nearly 24.7 years for the youngest cohort. Since C.EY consists of the sum of the 'hours per week'-specific subprofiles, it is of interest to determine which profile contributes most to the overall development. A closer look at Figure 2.B.3 shows that the increase in C.EY values is the result of a decrease in full-time employment and a relatively sharp increase in part-time employment. As far as the former is concerned, the $C.EY_{\geq 32h}$ values fell slightly from 11.9 years to 11.5 years. The decline is almost totally explained by sharply decreasing full-time participation rates at ages under 30. Within the group of part-time workers, the sharper increase can be found in $C.EY_{1-19h}$, the category of women working less than 20 hours per week, with respective values of 2.1 years and 7.7 years. Comparable numbers for $C.EY_{20-31h}$ are 1.9 years and 5.5 years. A combination of these figures shows that the proportion of part-time work in overall employment will double from 25% (1930-1932 cohort) to 53% (1963-1965 cohort). In this respect, the position of Dutch women may be considered quite exceptional.

The analysis of employment profiles so far has been based on participation in persons, aggregated into the average number of years spent by women in a given cohort in a paid job, regardless of the actual duration of the work week. From this point of view, a woman that works only 8 hours per week makes the same contribution to the value of C.EY as a colleague working the full 40 hours. As the proportion of part-time work in the Netherlands is quite substantial, it is appropriate to calculate a quantity that takes into account differences in working hours. This quantity, C.EPY, expresses employment in so-called person-year equivalents.

A sample of the results is depicted in Figure 2.2.2. It is obvious that only a relatively small part of the (theoretical) female employment potentials have been, or will be utilized. For the oldest cohort, the gross percentage is about 26%, whereas the youngest cohort scores 34%.[5] The figure also makes clear that C.EY and C.EPY values are, generally speaking, parallel for the younger cohorts, but then diverge. Taken as a whole, the growth of C.EY (56%) is sharper than the growth of C.EPY (32%).

Period observations
The simulation results of the transversal analysis are graphically presented in Figure 2.B.4 (Appendix B) and Figure 2.2. Looking at the period as a whole, it can be observed that in the first half (1960-1974), the profiles are rather stable and no major changes have taken place (Figure 2.B.4). Part-time participation rates are low, with a top value of about 10% in the 20-22 age group, and are almost zero after the age of 40. In the second part of this period, however, a steadily widening gap between overall participation and full-time participation emerges, showing a rapid increase in part-time work. As far as the latter is concerned, differences between women working 1-19 hours and 20-31 hours per week are only minor. In addition, age-specific part-time participation rates are remarkably constant, and are almost straight lines over the whole age span.

In Figure 2.2.3, a selection of employment profiles is brought together in order to illustrate the overall evolution in the period 1960-1995. As already observed in the longitudinal data, the peak of the curve has gradually shifted from the 20-22 age group to the 23-25 age group, which is an obvious consequence of prolonged education. This figure also shows the caesura in the employment profiles appearing after 1975. In the first part of the period described, about 60% of Dutch women worked either full-time or part-time; this percentage quickly dropped after their childbearing years to a modest level of 20-25%. In the last part of this period, the maximum participation rate fell to about 50%, but overall participation rates are almost double: the intensity value (the surface under the curve) increased from 12.3 years in 1960-1962 to 19.5 years in 1993-1995. This increase, however, is clarified by sharply rising part-time participation rates. Full-time participation even decreased slightly from 10.5 years to 9.2 years. The sharpest growth can be measured for women working 1-19 hours per week (from 0.7 years to 5.9 years), while in the remaining category (20-31 hours), an increase from 1.2 years to 4.4 years can be observed. Summarizing the data in a different way, we see that the proportion of part-time work in the overall participation rates has risen from 15% in 1960-1962 to 53% in 1993-1995. Comparable figures can be found in Emancipatieraad (1994) and Haller & Hoellinger (1994). According to cross-sectional Eurostat data for 1989, presented by Bernhardt (1993), 60% of all employed

---

[5]   These percentages have been calculated by dividing the cohort's Y.PPY value by the age interval 17-64 years. When narrowing the interval, percentages do, of course, increase.

Figure 2.2: Employment: cohort versus period observations

2.2.1 C.EY: 4 cohorts

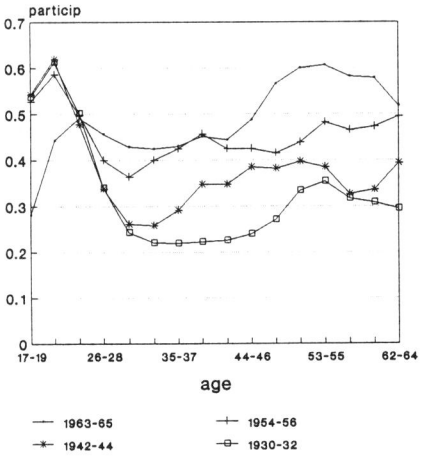

2.2.2 C.EY and C.EPY cohort observations

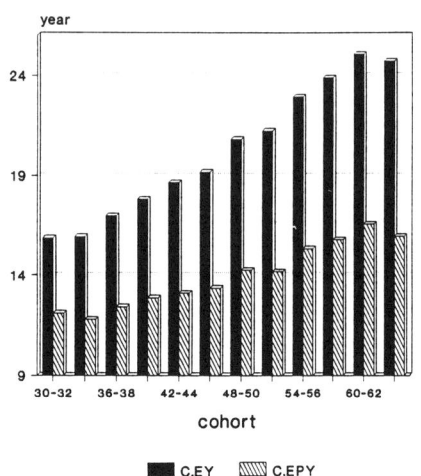

2.2.3 P.EY: 4 periods

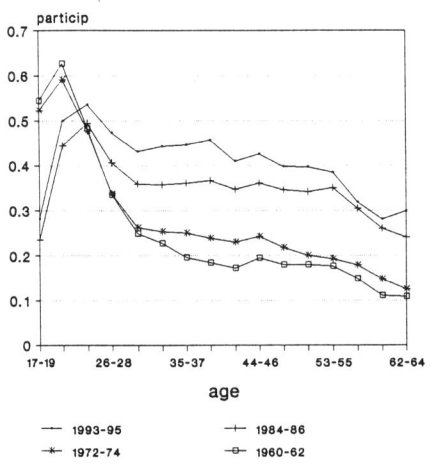

2.2.4 P.EY and P.EPY

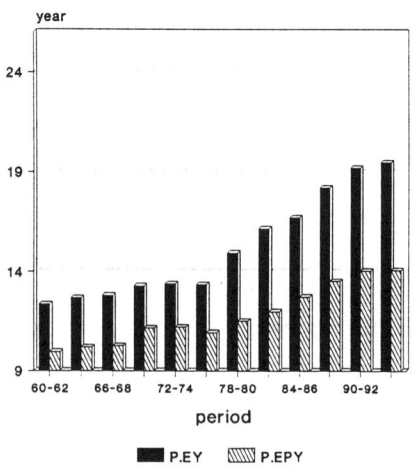

women in the Netherlands in the 25-44 age group, worked part-time, whereas the average percentage of all (12) members of the European Union was only 28%.

Another way to establish the ratio of part-time to full-time work is by comparing the development of P.EY (participation in persons) and P.EPY values (participation in person-years) as was done for the longitudinal data. In Figure 2.2.4, we see the result of this comparison. In the first part of the period, we observe a rather stable relationship between P.EY and P.EPY: both lines run almost parallel. However, afterwards employment in persons increases more sharply than employment in person years. For the period as a whole, P.EPY rises from 10.0 years (1960-1962) to 14.0 years (a 40% growth rate), while in the same period, P.EY witnessed a growth from 12.3 to 19.5 years (a 59% growth rate). In terms of the quantity 'female employment potentials' (dividing actual P.EPY by the theoretical maximum of 48 years), an incline is observed from 20.8% to 29.2%. Approximately the same figures, based on different data, are observed by Pott-Buter (1993, p. 205).

Employment profiles: a review

The comparison of female employment profiles from both time perspectives is more complicated than a comparison of longitudinal and transversal motherhood profiles. Part of the difficulty stems from the very nature of the employment profile. Contrary to the more biologically determined phenomenon of fertility, which leads to rather stable and age-bound patterns and closely follows a normal distribution, age-specific employment figures generally lack this kind of natural determination, and, as a consequence, are affected more by external influences like labour market situations, social norms, and governmental regulations. This is particularly obvious in the case of our longitudinal analysis, where employment profiles for the more recent cohorts are, for the most part, based on projections (that anticipate, among other things, future labour demand shortages), rather than on (factual) observations. Another related factor is that comparisons between longitudinal and transversal data cannot be based on the informal translation rule that was applied to motherhood data connecting cohorts and periods with a generation distance of about 30 years, approaching the average age of motherhood. Due to a greater variance and irregularities in the profile's shape, the average age of employed women is not an appropriate indicator of the variable in question. All in all, a precise comparison between cohort and period data is less meaningful, which is why we will restrict ourselves to a few general remarks based on Figure 2.2.

Let us first review the trend in EY and EPY values. From the cohorts' view, the percentage of women participating in paid work will grow by 56%, while the percentage of person-year equivalents (C.EPY) lags far behind (32%). This simply means that the proportion of part-time working women will increase in the future. Period data (1960-1995) show a rise of 59% in P.EYP values and of 40% in P.EPY values. For the last cohort under study (1963-1965), that is women who are now 28-30 years of age, this means that, according to current labour supply forecasts, on average almost 25 years of their life will be spent in the workforce. Expressed as full-time equivalents, women from this cohort will, on average, work 16 years of the theoretical 'potentially active' time span of (65-17=) 48 years. For the most recent period, comparable values of 19.5 and 14 years respectively were obtained.

Motherhood and employment: a dual career dilemma?

One of the aims of this contribution is to clarify the development of the 'combination' model in the Netherlands. Indeed, we are searching for the temporal origins of the dual career dilemma of Dutch women: the point at which they started combining motherhood with paid employment.

The competitive character of the relation between fertility and work has been phrased concisely by Regan and Roland (1985, p. 986) as follows: '... the timing of critical career-building phases does not accommodate women's biological life cycle.' Other authors mention incompatibilities or even an antagonistic relationship. The main characteristic of a dilemma situation is that individuals have to make choices between options that are equally valued but mutually incompatible. So, a dilemma is a predominantly psychological concept and should, therefore, preferably be studied at the micro level. However, as will be shown, our macro data can be used to elucidate some time aspects of the dilemma situation. Our data can offer a historical perspective, in the form of time series, on the rise and development of working mothers. To this end we will use the transversal data, which are, in this case, more reliable since they have not been influenced by 'external' economic and demographic projections. We will focus our attention on the development of two indicators of motherhood and employment: (1) the 'average number of years spent as the mother of a younger child' (P.MY) and (2) the 'average number of years spent in a paid job' (P.EY). It will be clear that an interpretation of this relationship at the individual (or micro) level is not allowed, since it could lead to ecological fallacies.

Since data on the realization of dual careers in the form of time series are not available, we will approximate this variable using the quantity P.EY, which expresses the participation volume of females. The use of the P.EY time series as an indicator of the evolution of the 'realization of dual careers' can be justified as follows. In the first place, the growth in female participation in the last three decades is mainly the result of the increasing participation of married women. The proportion of women who stay childless has remained fairly constant, especially over the last twenty years. By combining these two factors we can infer that the change in P.EY over time gives an acceptable indication of the numerical evolution of dual careers.

In Figure 2.3, we combine the trajectories of P.EY and P.MY$_{0-5}$ for the period 1960-1995, as determined in the previous sections. Two different periods can be distinguished: 1960-1975 and 1975-1995. At the beginning of the first period, P.MY and P.EY are relatively close together, representing elements of the traditional breadwinner pattern (Niphuis-Nell & Brouwer, 1995). During this period, a small but constant proportion of the women had paid work, in spite of the decline in time spent caring for young children. Apparently, these women were highly motivated to enter the labour market.

Figure 2.3: Motherhood and employment 1960-1965

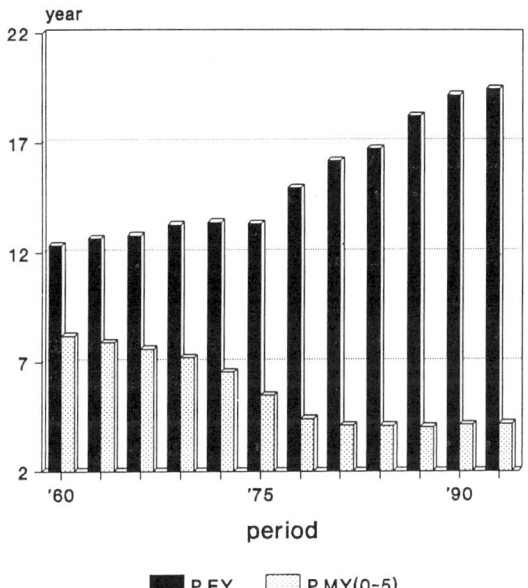

In the second period (1975-1995), the picture is now completely reversed. P.MY$_{0-5}$ has reached low and relatively stable values, while at the same time labour participation has sharply increased. A growing number of women with young children remained in or re-entered the labour market after the birth of their last child. Such a development reflects important societal shifts towards the creation of part-time work in the eighties and a rapid expansion of child care facilities in the nineties. However, the emergence of this new pattern of dual careers, combining a part-time job with a small family, reflects some difficult choices. In looking for a compromise between work and family, a growing number of women have decided to accept part-time work in order to have a family. Under these circumstances there may be no other choice.

Discussion

There is a general understanding that having children influences the labour force participation of women. The exact nature of this relationship, however, is still a subject of animated discussion. In this contribution we focused primarily on the question whether a longitudinal or transversal description of motherhood and employment would yield different historical patterns. The main concepts of motherhood and employment were operationalized in age-specific profiles, thus enabling the measurement of both intensity and timing aspects of the processes under study.

In the introduction we referred to the proposition that '... social change can be better understood by looking at the life histories of successive generations and cohorts,' due to the fact that '... cohorts are indelibly marked by their particular socialization throughout their existence in the system.' To what extent do our results support this view? If a better understanding of social change, and here we consider motherhood and employment careers to be exponents of social change, is indicated in terms of consistency in behaviourial patterns at the intra-cohort/intra-period level, the proposition is confirmed by our analysis. This is especially the case for motherhood careers. We found that birth cohorts yielded a much stronger consistency in the theoretically expected relationship between the average number of years spent as the 'mother of a young child' at different ages of the child ($C.MY_{0-5} > C.MY_{6-11} > C.MY_{12-17}$). This observation proves that a real cohort, as a unit of analysis, is more homogeneous (which might be explained by a commonly shared formation period) than a synthetic cohort, and in this respect better suited to the study of social change. When, on the other hand, we used *consistency* at the intra-cohort/intra-period level as a criterion rather than *regularity* at the inter-cohort/inter-period level, our initial expectations were confirmed. We have seen that the course of MY values for cohorts proceeds less smoothly than MY for periods. A straightforward explanation was not found.

As far as employment is concerned, we could say that period data yield more information about this indicator of social change than cohort data. P.EY as well as P.EPY values show a substantive rise after 1975, while at the cohort level, a structural disturbance is hardly visible. It can be concluded that, in this respect, cohorts as a unit of analysis are less informative than synthetic cohorts, or, in other words, period effects dominate cohort effects. In more general terms, it can be concluded that the proposition claiming that cohort analysis is superior for studying processes of social change, can be criticized in its absolute sense. It might be said that the predictive value of a shared formative period differs between social systems. As the case of female labour participation proves, Lindenberg's point of view that experiences in the formative period 'will show up even though it might be pushed around a bit by period effects and life cycle effects' (Lindenberg, 1992, p. 284) is obviously too rigid.

The view that cohort analysis is 'natural' and unconditionally superior, has been supported by a APC analysis of Dutch migration data by Mulder (1994), though Ní Brolcháin seriously criticized this type of analysis in the field of fertility (Ní Brolcháin, 1992).

In the final section, our data were used to find indications of the historical course of the dual career dilemma in the Netherlands. From this analysis we can conclude that the origin of the conflicts between motherhood and a professional career can be traced to the beginning of the sixties, marking the start of a period when the problem gradually worsened.

The principle of microsimulation is shown in Figure 2.A.1.2. To illustrate the general principle we will take the modelling of mortality. The decision whether an individual will or will not undergo a potential transition is simulated with the aid of the Monte Carlo method. To this end, the conditional probability of an individual undergoing that event has to be given. For example, for a 77-year-old widowed woman the probability of dying was 6.75 per cent in 1968. Subsequently, a number is randomly drawn from the uniform [0,1] distribution. If this number is smaller than or equal to the probability of dying of 0.0675, the woman is expected to die. If the number is larger, she will remain alive that year. If she dies, it is established whether she had children, and if so, they become orphans. So, decisions or events at an individual level can have implications for other individuals.

The heart of microsimulation modelling is formed by its state representation of the components of the system of interest. This is executed by drawing up a list of attributes for each individual in the sample. The next step, after the adaptation of a micro-representation, is the specification of an initial population. Preferably a real sample of individuals and households along with their attributes is used. However, such a sample was not available. A preliminary usable sample was derived from the Dutch 1947 Census data; see Nelissen (1994). The model simulates all events from 1947. Each year the characteristics of the individuals (and thus the households) are updated, if necessary.

The *demographic module* of NEDYMAS, from which the motherhood profiles were generated, contains 16 submodules. Each year starts with the determination of the number of immigrants. Next, all individuals successively go through the processes of family reunification (migrants), emigration, and return immigration. Thereafter the outflow out of institutional households has been simulated. Then the population in our database are subjected to the possibility of moving into an institutional household, death, being a candidate for marriage, divorce, dehabitation and being a candidate for cohabitation. When all persons are dealt with, the matching of persons takes place to complete the simulation of marriage and cohabitation. The last step in each year is the simulation of splitting-off children and fertility. The various transition rates are based on observations, if available. However, especially for the period 1947-1965, additional assumptions had to be made. The future demographic transition rates are based on the forecasts of the Netherlands Bureau of Statistics.

The data used to construct the employment profiles are generated by the *labour market and income module* of NEDYMAS. Labour supply is determined by a labour supply equation, modelled by Van Soest, Woittiez and Kapteyn (1990), which explicitly takes account of demand side restrictions. The labour supply of individual household members is considered in a neo-classical framework, in which after-tax wages, the social security and tax system, as well as the household composition, are taken into account. The Labour Force Surveys (Arbeidskrachtentellingen) are the starting point for the determination of the transition probabilities between the different states of economic activity. The states used in the Labour Force Survey are transformed into six states: disabled, employed, unemployed, soldier, student, and retired or working in own household. Using these data, it is determined for each year for each individual whether his or her economic activity has changed. For this process, additional data (e.g., unemployment data) are used. Future developments concerning labour participation and unemployment are based on forecasts of the Dutch Department of Social Affairs. It was assumed that national income will grow 2% per annum.

Monte Carlo variability

The (randomly selected) figures 2.A.1.3 and 2.A.1.4 give an indication of what is called the Monte Carlo variability (see Nelissen, 1994). They show simulation results of 8 runs, each with a different seed for the random generator. Figure 2.A.1.3 presents the outcome regarding the presence (or absence) of children, while Figure 2.A.1.4 contains simulation results concerning elements of the employment profile. As one can see, the variance resulting from the simulation approach appears to be rather limited. A more detailed and critical comparison of simulated data with observed data can be found in Nelissen (1991) and (1993).

Figure 2.A.1: Microsimulation: design and tests

fig 2.A.1.1 time scheme of analysis

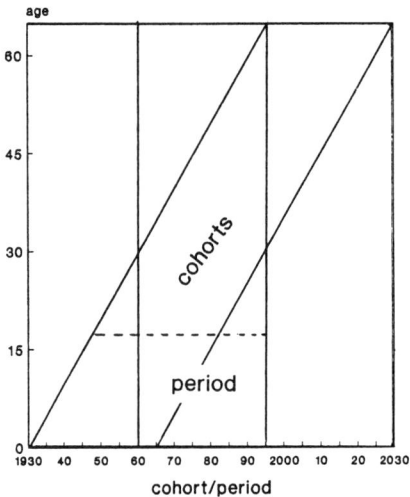

fig 2.A.1.2 principle of microsimulation

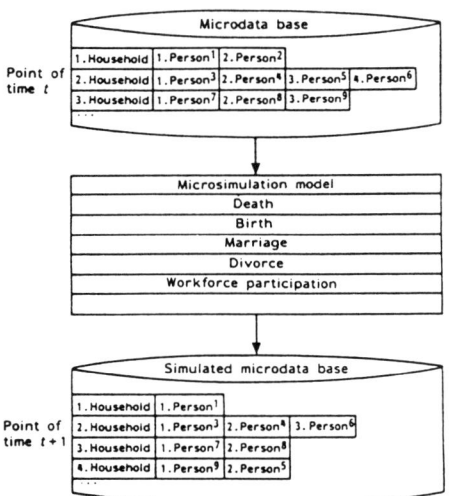

fig 2.A.1.3 motherhood profile
8 runs: period 1978-80 (0-5y)

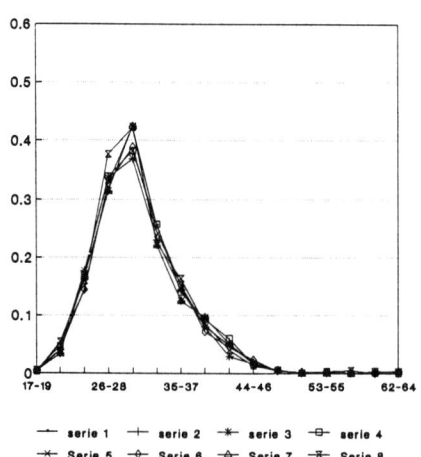

fig 2.A.1.4 employment profile
8 runs: period 1978-80 (>32h)

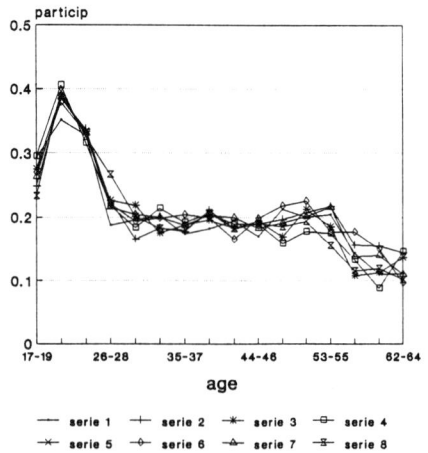

APPENDIX B: ADDITIONAL FIGURES

Figure 2.B.1: Motherhood profiles: cohort observations

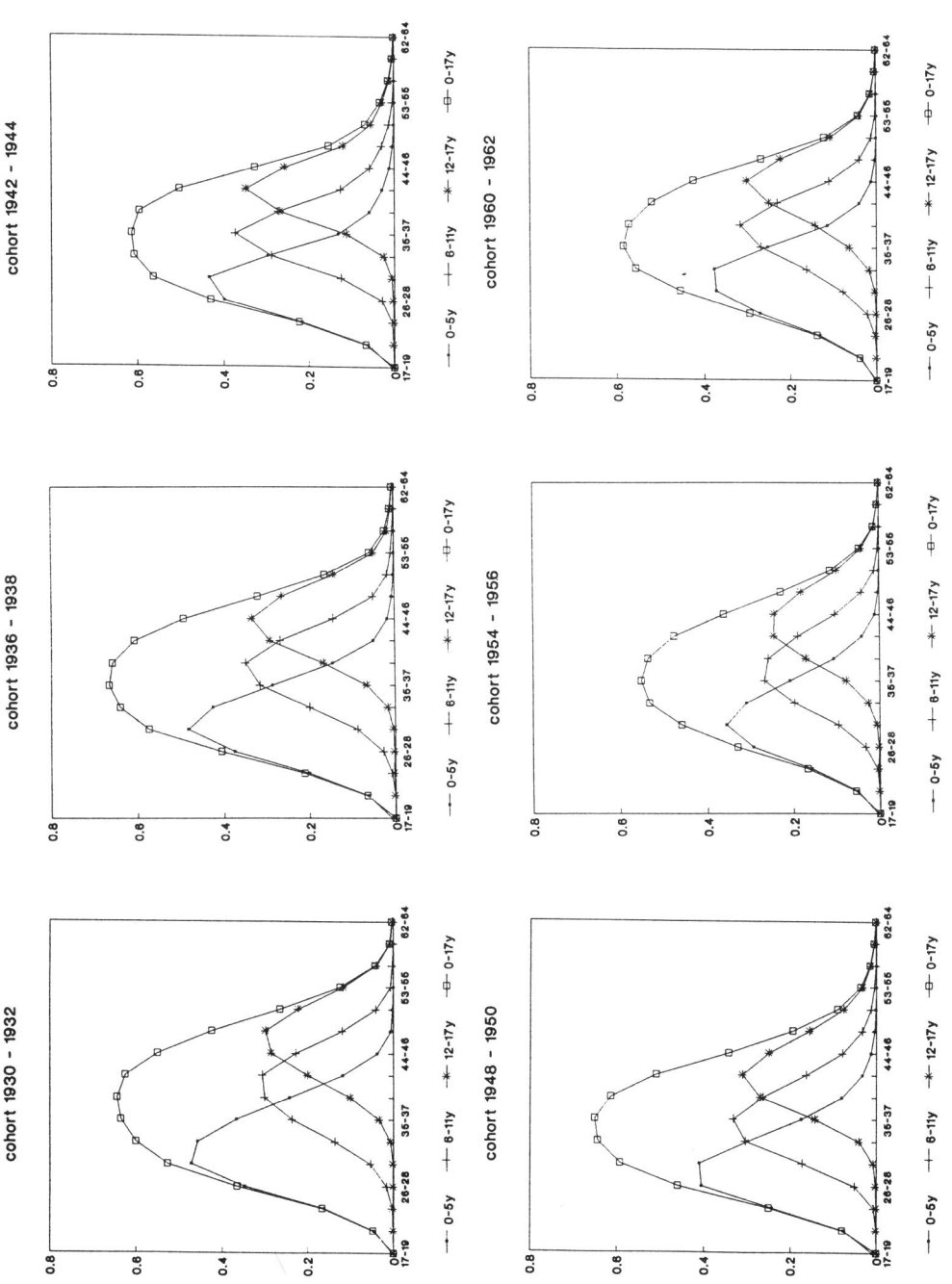

Figure 2.B.2: Motherhood profiles: period observations

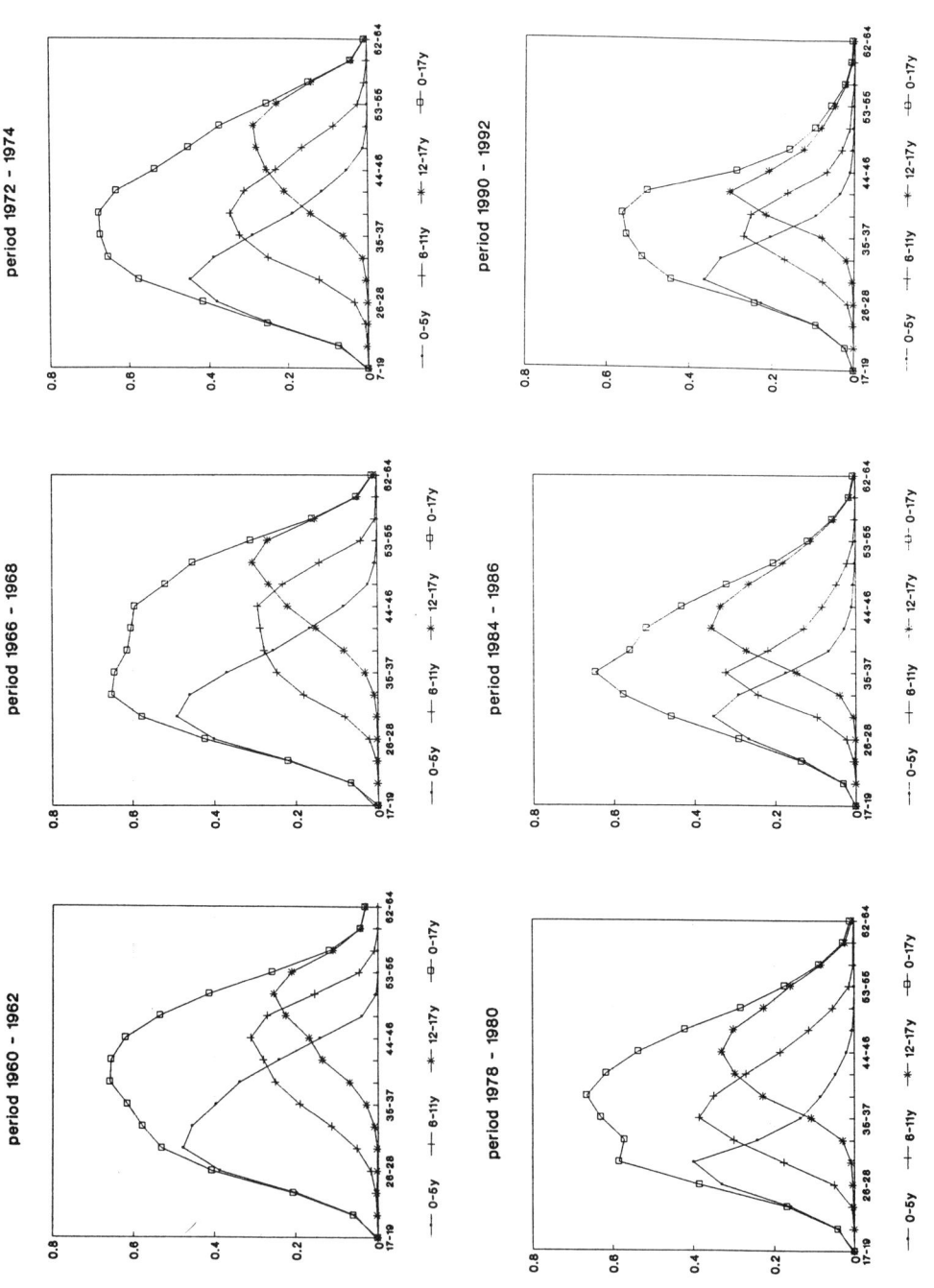

Figure 2.B.3: Employment profiles: cohort observations

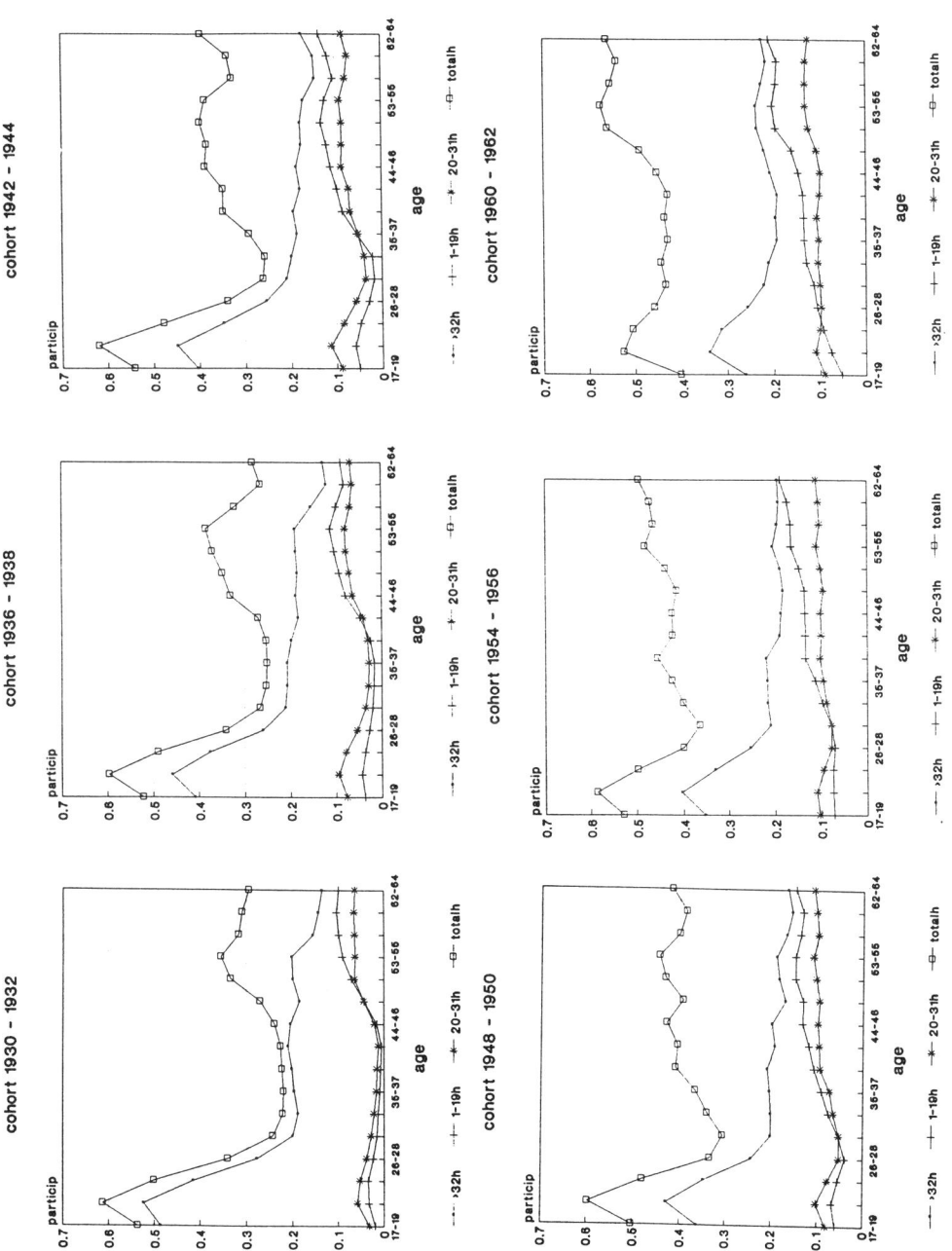

Figure 2.B.4: Employment profiles: period observations

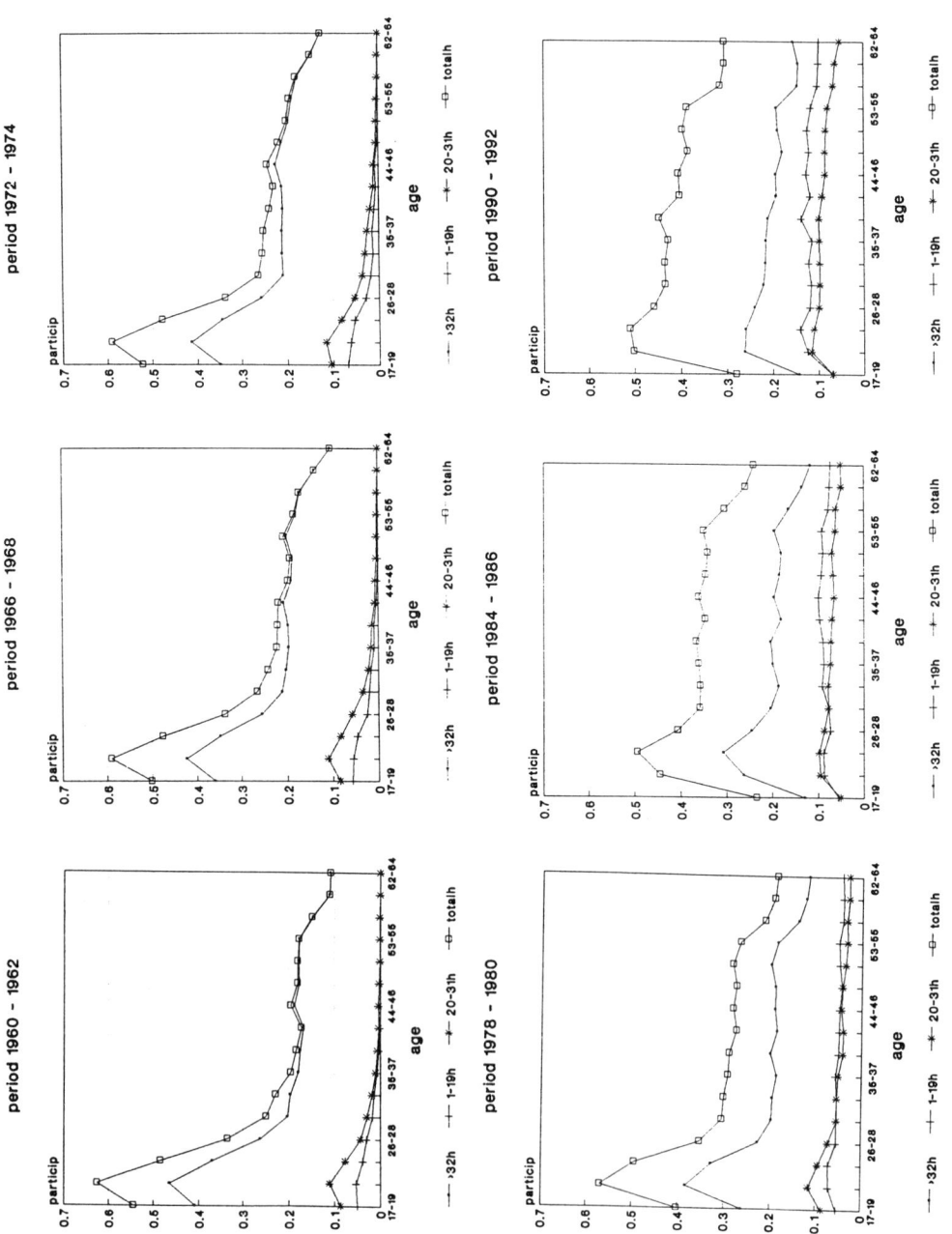

References

Becker, H.A. (1992). A pattern of generations and its consequences. In H. Becker (Ed.), *Dynamics of Cohort and Generations Research*. Proceedings of a symposium held on 12, 13 and 14 December 1991 at the University of Utrecht, The Netherlands. pp. 219-248. Amsterdam: Thesis Publishers.

Beets, G. (1993). Demographic trends: the case of The Netherlands. In N. Van Nimwegen, J.C. Chenais & P. Dykstra (Eds.), *Coping with sustained low fertility in France and The Netherlands*. pp. 13-42. NIDI CBGS Publications. Amsterdam: Swets & Zeitlinger.

Bernhardt, E. (1993). Fertility and employment. *European Sociological Review, Vol.1, May 1993*, 25-42.

Blossfeld, H.P. (1992). Birth cohorts and their opportunities in the Federal Republic of Germany. In H. Becker (Ed.), *Dynamics of Cohort and Generations Research*. Proceedings of a symposium held on 12, 13 and 14 December 1991 at the University of Utrecht, The Netherlands. pp. 97-138. Amsterdam: Thesis Publishers.

Bonsall, P. (1979). Micro-simulation of Mode Choice: a Model of Organized Car Sharing. *Planning and Transportation Research Conference Proceedings*, pp. 81-103.

Citro, C.F. & E.A. Hanushek (Eds.) (1991). *Improving Information for Social Policy Decisions. The Uses of Microsimulation Modelling*, vol. I and II, Washington D.C.: National Academy Press.

Emancipatieraad (1994). *Mannen die van meer markten thuis zijn*. Den Haag.

Hagenaars, J. (1990). *Categorical longitudinal data. Loglinear panel, trend and cohort analysis*. Beverly Hills: Sage Publications.

Haller, M. & F. Hoellinger (1994). Female employment and the change of gender roles: the conflictual relationship between participation and attitudes in international comparison. *International Sociology, vol. 9, no.1*, 87-112.

Janssen, A.J.M. & A.P. Vossen (1986). Vruchtbaarheidsdaling en ontgroening: misleidend verleden en onzekere toekomst. *Sociale Wetenschappen, 30ste jaargang no 3*, 215-240.

Jones, E.F. (1982). Ways in which childbearing affects women's employment: evidence from the U.S. 1975 National Fertility Survey. *Population Studies, 36, no. 1*, 5-14.

Kaa, D.J. van der (1987). Europe's second demographic transition. *Population Bulletin, Vol. 42*, no.1, 1-57.

Klijzing, E., J. Siegers, N. Keilman & L. Groot (1988). Static versus dynamic analysis of the interaction between female labour force participation and fertility. *European Journal of Population, 4*, 97-116.

Lindenberg, S. (1992). Cohorts, social production functions and the problem of self-command. In H. Becker (Ed.), *Dynamics of Cohort and Generations Research* Proceedings of a symposium held on 12, 13 and 14 December 1991 at the University of Utrecht. The Netherlands. pp. 283-308. Amsterdam: Thesis Publishers.

Mason, W.M. & S.E. Fienberg (Eds.) (1985). *Cohort Analysis in Social Research*. New York: Springer.

Mertens, N.H.M., J.J. Schippers & J.J. Siegers (1992). De arbeidsparticipatie van de gehuwde vrouw en de gezinsopbouw: gedragen Nederlandse vrouwen zich anders dan Vlaamse vrouwen? *Bevolking en Gezin, (3)*, 105-129.

Mertens, N.H.M., A. van Doorne-Huiskens, J. Schippers & J. Siegers (1995). De lage arbeidsmarktparticipatie van moeders in Nederland: culturele normen versus gebrek aan faciliteiten. *Bevolking en Gezin, (1)*, 49-78.

Mulder, C. (1994). Cohortbenaderingen van migratie: wanneer zinvol? (Cohort approaches of migration: when?). *Bevolking en Gezin, 1994/1*, pp. 27-51.

Nelissen, J. (1991). Household and Education Projections by Means of a Microsimulation Model. *Economic Modelling, 8*, 480-511.

Nelissen, J. (1993). The Labour Market and Social Security Module in the Microsimulation model NEDYMAS. *Economic Modelling, 10*, 225-272.

Nelissen, J. (1994). *Income Redistribution and Social Security. An application of microsimulation.* London: Chapman & Hall.

Ní Bhrolcháin, M. (1992). Period paramount? A critique of the cohort approach to fertility. *Population and Development Review, 18, 4*, 599-629.

Niphuis-Nell, M. & I. Brouwer (1995). Policies for combining and redistributing paid and unpaid work: The case of The Netherlands. In T. Willemsen, G. Frinking & R. Vogels (Eds.), *Work and family in Europe: the role of policies.* pp. 129-150. Tilburg: Tilburg University Press.

OECD (1991). *Employment outlook 1991.* OECD: Paris.

Pott-Buter, H.A. (1993). *Facts and Fairy Tales about Female Labor, Family and Fertility. A seven-country comparison, 1850-1990.* Amsterdam: Amsterdam University Press.

Regan, M.C. & H.E. Roland (1985). Rearranging family and career priorities: professional women and men of the eighties. *Journal of Marriage and the Family, 47*, 985-992.

Ryder, N. (1965). The cohort as a concept in the study of social change *American Sociological Review, 30*, 843-861.

Ryder, N. (1980). Components of temporal variations in American fertility. In R.W. Hiorns (Ed.), *Demographic patterns in developed societies.* pp. 15-54. London: Taylor and Francis.

Siegers, J., J. de Jong-Gierveld & E. van Imhoff (Eds.) (1991). *Female Labour Market Behaviour and Fertility. A Rational-Choice Approach.* Berlin: Springer-Verlag.

Sociaal en Cultureel Planbureau (SCP) (1993). *Sociale Atlas van de vrouw. Deel 2 Arbeid, inkomen en faciliteiten om werken en de zorg voor kinderen te combineren* By: B. Hooghiemstra & M. Niphuis-Nell. Den Haag: VUGA.

Sociaal en Cultureel Planbureau (SCP) (1996). *Sociaal en Cultureel Rapport 1996.* Rijswijk: SDU Publishers.

Soest, A. van, I. Woittiez & A. Kapteyn (1990). Labor Supply, Income Taxes, and Hours Restrictions in The Netherlands. *Journal of Human Resources, 15 (3)*, 517-558.

Spitze, G. (1988). Women's employment and family relations: a review. *Journal of Marriage and the Family, 50*, 595-618.

Vossen, A. and J. Nelissen (1994). *Motherhood and employment in The Netherlands. A longitudinal trend study.* WORC PAPER 94.05.025/2; Tilburg University, The Netherlands.

Whelpton, P. (1949). Cohort analysis of fertility. *American Sociological Review,* 14, 735-749.

Wetenschappelijke Raad voor het Regeringsbeleid (WRR) (1990). *Een werkend perspectief: arbeidsmarktparticipatie in de jaren '90.* Den Haag: SDU.

3

Ambivalence regarding the desire for children

Heleen van Luijn

Introduction

In the early seventies, couples almost always had children. Though the number of children per family was decreasing dramatically due to better contraception, and the timing of the first birth was more planned, the desire to have children was rarely questioned (Mozes, 1989).

In the last two decades, however, important changes have taken place in the Netherlands. First, an increasing number of people are consciously choosing to remain childless. Among women born in 1940, around 10% never had children (Beets & Te Velde, 1994). For women born around 1980, that figure is expected to be 20% (Beets, 1992). In particular, voluntary childlessness is on the increase.

Second, more and more couples are delaying having their first child. At the end of the 1960's, women were 24.5 years old on average when they had their first child. Twenty-five years later that age is 28.6 years and is expected to continue rising (CBS, 1995). In 1993, nearly *one* in every three women between the ages of 35 and 40 had a child under six years old. In twenty years, according to the CBS, half the women in this age group will have a young child. This delay is, however, not without risk: after the age of 30, the chance of pregnancy decreases. For a growing number of women, therefore, delay means having to abandon the idea of children (Vermunt, 1993).

Motherhood is no longer self-evident, something that just 'happens'; it now involves making a conscious decision. What developments have caused ambivalence concerning family formation? The following factors play a part: changes in the perception of motherhood, contradictions in current culture and society which make it difficult for women to combine work outside the home with child rearing, the high work and career standards women set for themselves, the co-existence of 'old' and 'new' value systems of, for example, motherhood, and increased negotiation with a partner about the various aspects of the relationship including having children. In addition, the societal conditions enabling women (and men) to combine different roles have not kept pace. Regulatory measures (i.e., of the government) which might make it easier for women to have and raise children have only recently come into effect. This chapter presents the results of an investigation among women as to whether or not they wanted children.

After a short description of the research method, the extent, span, gravity, and nature of the ambivalence are discussed. Subsequently, the reasons why women do or do not wish to have children are presented. The social-demographical, personal, social, and societal factors related to this ambivalence will be examined, followed by some conclusions.

Methodology

In 1988 and 1989, a large-scale national survey was conducted by the Netherlands Institute for Social Sexological Research (NISSO) on the ambivalence of women in their desire for children. The study consisted of a quantitative and a qualitative component.

As part of the quantitative component, 1201 Dutch women between the ages of 20 and 40 were surveyed by means of a written questionnaire. With the help of this questionnaire, the degree of doubt surrounding the decision to have children and the importance of the various considerations were determined. By comparing women who, for the period of at least *one* year, do or did not know whether they want/wanted children ('doubters') with women who were not ambivalent, a number of social-demographic and personality features of doubters were established, as well as their work motivation and ambitions.

Subsequently, a second interview was held with 69 respondents who were identified as doubters during the first phase. These follow-up interviews supplemented the survey component and provided an opportunity to acquire more information. New aspects, such as the perception of uncertainty and the decision-making process could also be investigated.

The results, to be discussed in the following sections, are derived from the survey as well as the in-depth interviews.

Extent, span, gravity, and nature of the ambivalence

Nearly *one* in five women (18.4%) in the sample has had doubts at one time or another about having children; 83% of them have thought about the problem for *one* year or more. This means that 15.2% of women in this age category have deliberated for at least one year over their decision. There is quite a difference in the duration of the uncertainty. Most of the women had thought about it for three years or less. 37% had deliberated for more than three years. For some of these women, the decision-making process lasted six years or more. On average, the women had spent about three-and-a-half years confronting the issue.

The majority of the doubters (75%) experience the question of 'whether or not to have children' as a problem. Somewhat less than one-third consider it rather serious to very serious in nature. Nearly half of the women, at one time or another, felt there was no way out, and a little over one-third had to ignore the problem at some point; they felt stuck, unable to decide. Delay is frequently the result. Almost two-thirds have therefore postponed their decision.

Why women do not want children
All the women who had expressed uncertainty for at least one year were asked to indicate to what extent certain considerations played a role in not wanting a child. A number of

reasons were mentioned and, except for two, could be clustered into four factors using a principal components analysis:

(1) threat to independence and self-realization;
(2) material obstacles;
(3) intimidated by the responsibility of raising a child;
(4) partner does not want children or is unwilling to share enough in child care.

The percentages in Table 3.1 show the number of women for whom the designated reasons played a very important or rather important role in not wanting children. The factor loadings are also given.

Table 3.1: Factors and reasons why doubters would not want children

	Doubters (N = 183)	Factor loading
(1) Threat to independence and self-realization		
I want to keep my freedom to do whatever I want	55%	0.82
I find it difficult to balance a child with work and/or study	50%	0.69
I'm afraid I won't have enough time for friends	20%	0.82
(2) Material obstacles		
I have too little income	16%	0.83
I don't have suitable housing	16%	0.70
I'm afraid that a child will negatively affect my	5%	0.59
(3) Intimidated by the responsibility of raising a child		
I feel intimidated by the responsibility of raising a child	54%	0.73
I don't think it's wise to bring children into this world	42%	0.77
I don't think my health is good enough	7%	0.47
(4) Partner does not want a child or is not willing to share		
My partner does not want a child	15%	0.78
My partner is not willing to share enough of the child care	8%	0.71
(5) Other factors		
I don't know if I'll stay with my partner	11%	-
I don't have a partner	10%	-

In addition to the reasons mentioned in the survey, other sources of uncertainty came out during the in-depth interviews. Some women were worried that they do not have what it takes to be a good mother. For some, a good mother is always there or spends the whole day with their child. In short, she devotes a lot of time and attention to the child. This is not, however, something these women imagine themselves doing. Frequently they are afraid of not being able to muster the patience or that, once they have a child, they will, in fact, want to devote all their time and attention to it, though they also want to continue working. It seems that for these women a traditional view of motherhood, coupled with other factors, contribute to their uncertainty. Fear of pregnancy and birth, and a physically or mentally handicapped child also play a role for some women. In some cases this concern arises after seeing a film about childbirth or if there is a handicapped child in the immediate environment. Fear of the unknown and change in general, plus the need to play it safe are further reasons for ambivalence. Finally, a few women were concerned about whether they could handle caring for a child alone if their partner were no longer around.

Table 3.2: Why doubters would want a child

	Doubters (N=183)	Factor loading
(1) Stimulation, novelty, fun		
I think it would be fun to watch a child grow up	84%	0.85
I would like to experience pregnancy and childbirth	53%	0.72
I like kids	69%	0.64
(2) Partner wants a child or a child will enrich the relationship		
My partner would like a child	39%	0.88
I want to enrich my relationship with my partner	22%	0.84
(3) Relationships in a primary group, affection		
I want to give more meaning to my life	32%	0.74
I don't want to be alone in later life	24%	0.65
With a child, I'll really feel needed	20%	0.78
(4) Fear of becoming an outsider without a child		
I'm afraid I'll regret not having children	42%	0.62
I want a child because friends and contacts have children	26%	0.78

Why women want children
The percentages in Table 3.2 reflect the number of women for whom the reasons mentioned play a very important or rather important role in wanting a child. The final column again indicates the factor loading.

The reasons why doubters would want a child clustered around four factors:
(1) stimulation, novelty, fun;
(2) partner wants a child or a child will enrich the relationship;
(3) relationships in a primary group, affection;
(4) fear of becoming an outsider without kids.

Categorizing the doubters
The doubters could be broken down into several groups based on the most salient reasons for ambivalence derived from the in-depth interviews. The result is a global classification of the groups since not all of the women fit neatly into the categories. The classification presented below is therefore mainly based on the women's perceptions of the most relevant factors.

(1) women with a conflict between their personal desire for children and that of their partner
For 20% of the doubters (N=69), the woman's desire for children conflicts with that of her partner: either the woman herself wants a child and the partner does not, or the woman does not want a child while the partner does. In this case, the woman knows what she wants, but her partner's position prevents her from realizing her choice. In half of the cases, the woman wants a child; in the other half, the partner wants one.

(2) women who are anxious about combining children with work and/or study
For another 20%, the difficulty of balancing a child with work underlies their ambivalence. Besides loss of freedom, fear of being alone if the partner is no longer around, anxiety about the serious responsibility of child rearing, and worry about not being a good mother were given by some of the women in this group as important sources of uncertainty. For all these women, however, the emphasis was clearly on the child-work combination.

(3) women who worry about not being able to cope with having a child
For 18%, worry about not being able to cope with having a child and feeling intimidated by the serious responsibility involved in raising children were the main reasons for ambivalence.

(4) women who fear loss of freedom
A little over 13% expressed doubt because of the loss of freedom their choice would entail. Though this was mentioned by more than half the doubters as playing a role in their uncertainty, from the in-depth interviews it is clear that a much smaller number of women consider it a serious problem.

(5) women with other reasons
Finally, there is a fifth group of women who attributed their ambivalence to reasons other than those presented above. Examples of these are: fear of pregnancy and childbirth, doubts about their suitability as a mother, absence of a partner, and financial reasons.

Social-demographic, personal, social, and societal factors related to ambivalence

By comparing the women who had expressed doubts about wanting children for at least one year ('doubters') with the women who had no doubts, a large number of social-demographic, personal, social, and societal factors related to ambivalence were identified.

Social-demographic factors

Age
More than three-quarters of the undecideds (N=41) are 30 years of age or younger. The majority had doubts before the age of 35. We can therefore conclude that ambivalence does not occur exclusively among women in their late 30s. On the contrary, most of the women are confronted with the problem long before.

Marital status
Most of the undecided women cohabit with their partners. More than one-third have, at some time or another, had doubts about having children. Women with a LAT relationship and women without partners are also strongly represented among the undecideds (see Table 3.3).

Table 3.3: Marital status

	Doubts (N=183)	No doubts (N=790)	Total (N=973)
Married (N=728)	14%	86%	100%
Cohabiting with steady partner (N=98)	39%	61%	100%
Steady partner, not cohabiting (N=55)	33%	67%	100%
No partner (N=90)	26%	74%	100%

Educational level

Of the highly educated women, 41% are unsure about having children. This is more than twice as high as the middle category and five times greater than the less educated women. Ambivalence is mainly a problem of the highly educated (see Table 3.4).

Table 3.4: Educational level

	Doubts (N=183)	No doubts (N=790)	Total (N=973)
Low (N=271)	8%	92%	100%
Mid (N=537)	20%	80%	100%
High (N=137)	41%	59%	100%

Personal factors

Working outside the home, work motivation and ambitions

When we compare the group of women who expressed ambivalence at the time of the study (N=41) with women who were not uncertain and do not have children (N=136), we see that the doubters exhibit strong work ambitions; they feel it is more important to achieve at their jobs (t=2.32, p<.05). However, they do not have paid employment more often, nor do they or would they want to work more than non-doubters. The two groups also do not differ in the value they attach to having paid employment or in their motivation for working.

Views on gender roles and partner responsibility

Seven statements of an emancipatory nature were presented to all the women, with instructions to indicate the extent to which they agreed with these statements. Women who expressed doubts (N=41) were more in agreement with the statements than women who are not and never were ambivalent (N=790, t=-6.60, p<.001).

For example, 88% of the women who had doubts at the time of the investigation (N=41) judged it quite important to very important that their partner participate in a substantial share of the child care (68% rate it very important). The doubters attach greater importance to this than women who are not uncertain and do not have children (N=136, t=2.55, p<.05). Half of the women who expressed ambivalence also wanted their partners to work 30 hours per week or less if they had a child. Among non-doubters the figure was 21%. This is a significant difference (t=2.59, p<.05). A little more than half the doubters (58%) who favoured this arrangement felt their partner would also be supportive. One-quarter would want their partner to work between 32 and 39 hours per week and felt he would be willing to do so. More than three-quarters of the women who expressed ambivalence (N=41) wished to continue working if they had children (27 women); this figure is 41% for the non-doubters. For the majority, child care would ideally be taken care of with their partner so that outside help would not be necessary. Of those who see outside care as an ideal solution, the majority favour paid help at home. A day care centre or child care at work would also be ideal. During the in-depth interviews, the possibility of child care at the partner's work was also mentioned as a preferred solution.

It can be concluded that those women who expressed doubt at the time of the survey have less traditional views of gender role stereotypes: they attach greater value to closing the social and societal distance between men and women.

Independence in relationships

The degree of independence in the relationship was measured by three statements: (1) I often feel that I couldn't live without my partner; (2) Without my partner my life would not have much meaning; and (3) My partner is the driving force in my life. The doubters (N=41) more often disagreed with these statements than the non-doubters (N=136, $t=2.51$, $p<.05$; $t=4.40$, $p<.001$; $t=3.71$, $p<.001$). This indicates that doubters are less dependent on their partners.

Social factors

General sense of well-being and decisiveness

In order to investigate the general sense of well-being among the women, each of them was presented with twelve statements and asked to indicate how strongly they agreed or disagreed. The statements were not evaluated differently by the doubters and non-doubters. A difference in general level of contentment is therefore not a feature of the doubter group.

In the interviews, some of the doubters described themselves as insecure and anxious and some individuals felt they were not in an optimal phase of their lives. We have seen that, for some women, these factors are related to their ambivalence. Statements measuring the degree of decisiveness were not rated differently by ambivalent (N=41) and non-ambivalent women (N=136, $t=.73$, n.s.). Therefore, there is no difference between doubters and non-doubters in the extent to which they are prepared to make decisions.

Childhood experiences

Family experiences are relevant to the personal histories of the women. Although, strictly speaking, they are not considered social context factors, we address them here for the sake of comparison.

All the women were asked how they experienced their childhoods. Doubters (N=183) on average had a less positive experience than women who have not struggled with the ambivalence issue (N=790, t=4.18, p<.001). Approximately one-third of the doubters had a less than pleasant youth. Most of the women feel that their childhood experiences affected their ambivalence towards children. There were also women who had pleasant childhoods yet still feel it has played a part in their ambivalence. Some felt they had to think about difficult things too early in life. Also mentioned in this regard, were lack of support and having to make decisions too soon. Others were raised alone because of the large age difference between siblings and therefore do not know how to relate to small children. Still others (especially those from large families) had to settle for less financially because of family size and wonder whether they want to repeat the experience. Frequently, there is anxiety about making the same mistakes their parents did. This may also be due to fear of failure. The desire for attention that was denied in youth (for example in the case of a large family) is another reason some women choose not to have children. They are concerned that a child would get all the attention. Assuming responsibility in the family at too young an age (caring for younger brothers and sisters) can also mean, for some, that it's time to enjoy their freedom. Therefore, women who are experiencing or have experienced ambivalence (N=183) were more often the oldest child than women who do not or have not had doubts (N=790, t=-2.83, p<.01). Among the doubters, 39% were the oldest sibling; among the non-doubters, this figure is 28%. Women who are voluntarily childless were more often first or only children. However, doubters are not more likely to be only children.

Partner's desire for children
All women with a steady partner were asked, as part of the survey, whether their partner wanted children. Seven per cent of the partners of the doubter group want a child as soon as possible, 41% eventually want one, and 52% don't know. Among the non-doubters these figures are 20%, 72%, and 8%, respectively. More than half the doubters' partners expressed ambivalence themselves about children, while for the partners of the non-doubters the figure was only 8%. Doubters and non-doubters differ significantly on this point (t=-2.33, p<.05). Doubters (N=41) more often have a difference of opinion with their partners on this subject than non-doubters (N=136) (t=3.10, p<.01). This indicates a relation between the male partner's attitude toward having children and the woman's ambivalence.

Quality of the partner relationship
By far the majority of children are born within a relationship. If there are doubts about the relationship, if it is not stable or there are problems, there will also be uncertainty about having a child under these circumstances. If doubters have bad, unstable relationships, their

uncertainty may have to do with the relationship rather than personal or societal factors. With this in mind, the quality of the relationship with the partner was investigated and four statements on the degree of conflict avoidance within the relationship were presented to the women with steady partners.

On the basis of a t-test, no significant difference was found between the doubters and non-doubters in their tendencies toward conflict avoidance in the relationship, nor in their level of satisfaction over the division of household tasks.

Societal context factors

Government policy

In the survey, the doubters (N=183) were asked to what extent changes in certain governmental regulations relevant to having and raising children would influence their decision to have children. Since the non-doubters were not surveyed on this point, comparison was not possible.

The particular option of more part-time jobs for men would, for more than half the doubters, make it easier to choose for having children. Parental leave, expansion of child care services, and extension of pregnancy leave (at the time of the survey 12 weeks, currently 16 weeks), would definitely or probably affect a large number of doubters' (25-56%) decisions to have a child. This confirms the emancipatory inclinations of the doubters and points out the importance of government policy in reducing the ambivalence problem.

Background factors and ambivalence

In order to gain more insight into the independent contribution of the background factors in clarifying ambivalence, a multivariate logistic regression analysis was performed on the factors significantly associated with ambivalence. The dependent variable was the presence or absence of ambivalence. The analysis was done for women who expressed uncertainties (N=41) and non-doubters without children (N=136). Because no data on work ambition and independence in the relationship were collected for women without steady partners who did not work outside the home, the analysis was conducted on only 115 women. Two analyses were performed. The first concerned the personal factors and personal history (childhood experience) of the woman. The results are presented in Table 3.5. The second analysis was performed for all factors found to be significantly related to ambivalence. As shown in Table 3.5, only childhood experience and the degree of independence in the partner relationship were significant: these factors taken together are the best predictors of ambivalence. Therefore, a woman's degree of independence in her relationship as well as less pleasant childhood experiences best explain an ambivalent attitude towards having children. If the analysis is not limited to the woman's significant individual factors and personal history, but includes the significant social context factors as well, another picture emerges. If we add the 'partner's desire for children' to the analysis, this proves to be the only significant factor (B=-3.896, p=.003); childhood experiences and degree of independence in the relationship fall away. Therefore, a partner's ambivalence or negative desire for children is the best predictor of ambivalence in the woman. This underscores the significance of the partner's attitude with respect to having children as clarification of the ambivalence phenomenon. In interpreting the results, it is important to remember that doubters who do not work outside the home and do not have a steady partner were not included in these analyses.

Table 3.5: Results of the multivariate logistic regression analysis

Background factors	Doubters + Non-doubters (N=115)		
		B	p
Level of education			n.s.
Work ambitions			n.s.
Gender role views			n.s.
Independence in relationship		-.235	.04
Childhood experiences		-.923	.02
Oldest child in family			n.s.
Important that partner shares in child care			n.s.

Conclusion

The scope, duration, and severity of the ambivalence phenomenon demonstrate that it is a serious problem. The decision 'whether or not to have a child' causes long-term uncertainty in one out of six to seven Dutch women between the ages of 20 and 40: these women struggle with the problem an average of three-and-a-half years. For three-quarters of the women, this doubt constitutes a real problem and half have had the feeling that it can't be resolved. In balancing the perceived costs and benefits, the decision whether or not to have children poses a threat to the important life goals of these women.

We have seen that this issue is not so much a problem of women in their late thirties, but mainly of younger women: more than three-quarters of the doubters are 30 years of age or younger. Particularly women who cohabit, women with a LAT relationship and women without partners are strongly represented. A high level of education, serious career ambitions, low conformity to the rigid gender role stereotypes, and a high degree of independence in relationships distinguish this group. It can also be concluded that ambivalence concerning the decision 'whether or not to have children' mainly occurs among emancipated women. The general sense of well-being and the degree of decisiveness of these women is no different from women who express no ambivalence. Some of the women studied, however, did describe feelings of insecurity and a somewhat indecisive attitude. Furthermore, ambivalent women more often had a less pleasant childhood and were frequently the oldest children in the family. Doubters are also more likely than non-doubters to have partners who do not want children or are themselves in doubt. Finally, the majority of these women have good, stable relationships.

All this seems to indicate that sources of ambivalence are to be found in the advancing emancipation process, in the personal histories (childhood experiences) of the women, and in the attitudes of their partners with respect to having children. Particularly our finding concerning government initiatives which would make it more feasible for some women to choose for a child, supports the first conclusion. The findings that doubters more often had a less pleasant childhood and that some of the women described themselves as anxious, insecure, and indecisive, supports the second. These conclusions are confirmed by the results of the regression analyses where it became apparent that, of the personal factors, the degree of independence in the partner relationship and childhood experience are the best predictors of ambivalence; however, if we look at all the factors, the partner's ambivalence or negative desire for children is the single most important predictor. This indicates that personal and social as well as societal context factors are important for understanding the sources of ambivalence. However, the partner's undecided or negative attitude towards having children (social context) carries the most weight.

A change in attitude of the male partner and, to a lesser degree, an expansion of government regulations to facilitate the combination of working outside the home and child care, are expected to alleviate or lessen the ambivalence problem. Whether these changes in the immediate social environment of the woman and in the broader context of Dutch society will occur in the near future, remains to be seen.

Changes in the workplace and improvement in governmental policy to facilitate the combination of work and child care for women, are slow to come about. Increasing the participation of men in raising and caring for children is also a particularly slow process. This is due not only to the men themselves - according to various studies, many men would be willing to work part-time in order to share responsibility for child care - but also to the employers who advance economic arguments why part-time work is not feasible (cf. Pelzer & Miedema, 1992). At the same time, the aspirations of women are expected to grow: in addition to being mothers, they want to work outside the home and have time to pursue other activities.

Research in the Netherlands shows that boys and girls think very differently about the position of men and women in the work force and in the family (Du Bois-Reymond, 1992). Boys have a traditional outlook on the future in these matters. Three-quarters of the boys studied expect to have an uninterrupted full-time career, even when they have children. They believe their partner should be responsible for the child care. In contrast, less than half the girls expect to have continuous part-time work. Approximately one-fifth expect a temporary interruption in their careers while they are raising young children. Slightly less than half expect to stop working completely with the birth of their first child. Boys are less concerned about the 'work, career, and child' dilemma than their potential future female partners. They do not consider the combination of parenthood and a (full-time) career a problem, but simple reality. The doubts and dilemmas that women face are therefore not likely to abate in the near future.

References

Beets, G. (1992). Kinderen krijgen in de 20e eeuw. In G.C.N. Beets & P. Verloove-Vanhorick (Eds.), *Een slimme meid regelt haar zwangerschap op tijd.* Amsterdam/Lisse: Swets & Zeitlinger B.V.

Beets, G. & E. Te Velde (1994). Op oudere leeftijd nog een kind? De gevolgen van uitstel en de rol van medische hulp. *Demos, 10*, 1-5.

Bois-Reymond, M. du (1992). Werk, ouderschap en toekomst van jongeren: het gezin-carrière dilemma. In H.J. Bronsema & R.F. van der Erf (Eds.), *Emancipatie en Bevolkingsontwikkeling. Hechte partners?* Den Haag: Nederlandse Vereniging voor Demografie.

CBS (1995). Jaarcijfers geboorte 1990-1994. *Maandstatistiek van de bevolking, 95/10*, 22-31.

Mozes, M. (1989). *Uitstel of afstel. Kiezen voor kinderen in een veranderende samenleving.* Culemborg: Lemma.

Pelzer, A. & N. Miedema (1990). *Kinderopvang in Nederland, de FNV-enquête.* Amsterdam: Stichting FNV-pers.

Vermunt, J.K. (1993). De geboorte van het eerste kind: uitstel of afstel? *Gezin, 5*, 31-52.

4

Strategies for combining work and children

Thérèse van den Heuvel
Monique Turkenburg

Introduction

The overall pattern in the past decades showed that most Dutch women treated the activities of work and childrearing as sequential. Nowadays more and more women strive for a combination of the two. In the last twenty years, the labour market participation of women with (small) children has increased dramatically. In 1992, 53% of women continued working after the birth of their first child (SCP, 1994, p. 41). This pattern of work and care behaviour is particularly prevalent amongst highly educated women (Tijdens, Maassen van den Brink, Noom & Groot, 1994). Other women stop working, but return to the labour market after having taken care of their children and household for some years. In general, this pattern is followed by women with lower levels of education. Women who stopped working and did not intend to return to paid labour are also generally less educated (Tijdens et al., 1994). Nonetheless, the labour market participation of women with low levels of education and small children is increasing as well.

But even if the two categories of women follow the same pattern, there are still striking differences in the factors that shape and determine their combination strategies. These factors are often cumulative and are somehow linked to level of education, such as the kind of jobs held, motherhood and work aspirations, and the opportunities and constraints that make a satisfactory combination of work and childrearing possible.

This chapter focuses on a group of women born between 1945 and 1961, and examines how differences in educational level affect the two groups in their efforts to combine paid work and childrearing. We will look at their strategies for making this combination possible. The comparison is based on our separate studies on the choices of women with a low level of education between a job and/or a child and on the work histories of women with high levels of education respectively. Table 4.1 shows the main features of these studies.

The question we will try to answer here concerns the differences and similarities in the strategies women with low and high levels of education use in order to successfully combine paid work and child care. These strategies are practical and consist of choosing a suitable labour market participation pattern: working part-time; sharing care and household tasks within the family; looking for child care facilities; and contracting out the household tasks.

Table 4.1: Short outline of the two studies

	sample 1: Van den Heuvel (unpublished)	sample 2: Turkenburg (1995)
Education level	high	low
Main subject of study	work histories of highly-educated women	job and/or child aspirations & strategies of less-educated women
Number of women	N=56 (in survey)	N=54
Women with children	35 mothers	47 mothers
Women interviewed	14 interviewed	54 interviewed
Sources	- written questionnaire - face to face in-depth	- secondary analysis of survey sample - written form - face to face in-depth
Birth cohorts	1945-1955	1950-1961
Labour market patterns	continuous and discontinuous workers	quitters, continuous and discontinuous workers

Strategies: between preferences, possibilities and constraints

The following macro-level changes in employment behaviour have occurred: more women, even those with less education, are following a combination pattern, indicating that we should perhaps treat the commonly known determinants that are linked to educational level or differences in employment behaviour more carefully. The most general explanation for combining work with childrearing is to be found in the market skills women have. According to some researchers, job satisfaction is more likely to be experienced by highly educated women. The more women expect higher wages, the more professionally experienced they are, the older and the more educated they are, the more likely they are to continue to work after the birth of their first child. Most social and economical explanations concentrate on these differences in human capital. But there are other possible and equally plausible explanations.

The central issue is whether the 'old' human capital-like explanations for differences in employment behaviour after the first birth, still hold true now that more women (including those with less education) follow this combination pattern. Do women make rational calculations or make side bets when remaining employed? Do less educated women work solely for the money, and should we interpret their behaviour more in terms of some sort of extended motherhood aspirations (more family income to meet the needs of growing children) than in terms of self-realization?

To answer these questions we need to know whether a certain strategy should be interpreted in terms of choice and preference or dictated by the limited possibilities of combining a job with having children. These possibilities may vary structurally for women with different levels of education, but can also vary among individuals. We therefore need to be aware of the 'objective' as well as the 'subjectively perceived' opportunities and constraints. All too often the wishes and preferences of women are - sometimes perhaps for political reasons - left out of the picture. Generally speaking, in social research more attention is paid to the outcome (the patterns these women follow) than on the complex and ongoing process of wishes, choices, opportunities, and constraints that make women shape and reshape their strategies. However, to gain more insight into possible shifts and changes in the strategies used by women of all educational levels, it is fundamental to make, wherever possible, a clear distinction between what women want and the structural problems they face in realizing their ideal combination. Only then can we answer a question like: Are highly educated women trend-setters to be followed by less educated women?

We will now look into the practical solutions the women in our samples have found in combining employment with family tasks.

Working part-time

In the Netherlands more than in any other country, women (prefer to) work part-time. This is the main solution for combining care and paid work. Of the women with underaged children, only 7% work more than 35 hours a week (Ministerie van Sociale Zaken en Werkgelegenheid, 1995). According to this figure, women of all educational levels with younger children to care for, prefer to work part-time. But the opportunities for part-time work and the types of part-time jobs available are not the same for highly and less educated women.

Highly educated women often have more autonomy and flexibility in their jobs and can therefore better arrange their working hours. Besides, the jobs they look for and eventually hold offer these opportunities. Particularly employment in the education sector provides them with working hours and schedules compatible with caretaking tasks and responsibilities. That is why more than half of the highly educated women in sample 1 currently hold or have held an educational job. Most of them work less than the usual number of hours, but even full-time work is possible:

'Because of the children I have chosen a job where a part of the working hours can be worked
at home.'
(Teacher at a college for higher education, two children, working full-time)

There is little objection to part-time work, not only in the education sector but also in other
sectors, where many highly educated women work. However, for these women, it means
that the choice of jobs is limited to these sectors, as are the career opportunities. Choosing
a job which offers opportunities for part-time work generally means limiting the chance of
further growth.

'Reducing working hours is at the expense of influence and responsibilities in a position.'
(Management consultant, two children, working 30 hours)

However, for most women, being able to combine work and family by working part-time
was more important than a career. For some women, reducing working hours was not easy.
Because they had worked several years for the same employer and were very persistent,
they were allowed to work one day less, but no more. As the only part-time employees they
are looked upon as that 'part-time woman.' The consequences are that:

'You are less available. I'm flexible in my hours, but not in the same way as before. I was
130% available then and that's been reduced to 80% and no more. That's difficult.'
(Secretary of an association of traders, two children, works 32 hours)

Many women say that it is not always easy to manage the workload in the available hours.
But, although working part-time meant making concessions, most highly educated women
did not have too many problems finding jobs with reduced working hours that were still
satisfactory.

The situation is different for women with fewer marketable skills and less education.
Their opportunities are more restricted. If and when they work part-time, it is often
something they had to fight for. It was not an institutionalized or job-related alternative.
The women who claimed to have stopped working because they wanted to take care of their
children, often worked in places where no facilities or arrangements were available.
Individual solutions include bargaining tactics by women with their employers. Sometimes
they succeed, sometimes they don't. But the results of these negotiations are not always very
satisfactory. Although the women can continue working, their shifts and the contracts they
are offered are not what they would have preferred. Only highly motivated women put up
with this. Some women said they considered the arrangement temporary. For them it was
a strategy to keep their job. They continue looking for better options or more working hours
as they become available and as they become more able to commit themselves.

Not only do highly educated women have more and better opportunities for part-time work in a job they prefer, but it is almost always at least 20 hours per week with regular hours. Working part-time for less educated women more often means working less than 20 hours a week and on an irregular basis. Some women work full-time for one week, then stay home the next week. Others work in shifts. Several kinds of strategies for combining work and children are restricted to the job levels less educated women work at. All these strategies have their drawbacks. Working night shifts enables women to combine a job and children, but has physical side-effects and can put pressure on the couple.

Working at home is another strategy. This has certain advantages in combining childrearing and child caring tasks with work, but many of the women that chose this option want to return to a regular job outside the home. As for the co-workers, i.e., women who run a shop with their husbands or those who work on the family farm, the self-evidence of their work and the indirect 'payment' make it hard to look upon their work as a job. The risks of a divorce are perhaps most obvious for this category of women. One possible disadvantage of their - often long - working hours can be their 'invisibility.'

Sharing tasks with partners

As we have seen, first birth mothers in particular reduce their working hours, enabling them to combine work and care. But children have fathers as well. What is their part in the (increased) share of family household tasks?

On a macro level it can been seen that men who become fathers, in contrast with new mothers, increase their hours of paid work (Tijdens et al., 1994). Nevertheless, in the Netherlands, the percentage of men with underaged children who work in a part-time job is still only 7% (Ministerie van Sociale Zaken en Werkgelegenheid, 1995). However, it is not said that they use their spare time to take care of the children. Highly educated women in particular are beginning to negotiate for more symmetrical parenting (Morée, 1992). Some of them succeed, in which case both parents work part-time and have a more or less equal share in the care of their children. This does not go without saying. It is almost always the woman who has to take the initiative and entails ongoing negotiation. One woman who worked 20 hours and now has a job for 32 hours per week, made her husband work a day less. She had to convince him that she could earn enough money so his full-time income was no longer necessary.

'Now he's very positive about it. In fact he has no problem sharing the chores, the casualness of it. But he constantly says that it must not go too far, that he has his limits.'
(Quality manager, three children, works 32 hours)

Just as it is easier for women with teaching jobs to combine employment and child care, so it is for the spouses with a job in that field. Some highly educated women go to work when their partner works at home.

> 'My husband is a university teacher. He only goes to work to give lectures or attend meetings. So we manage easily, he's there or I'm there.'
> (Social worker, two children, worked 20 hours when the children were small)

But most highly educated women have husbands with very 'demanding' jobs, who have to work far more than 40 hours per week. Although most of them say that their partner looks after the children as well, the following comment is typical:

> 'My husband will always cover for me, when he is at home. But you can never count on his presence, and so managing the family is completely my responsibility.'
> (Physician, three children, working 20 hours)

A lot of less educated women would also like a form of symmetric parenting but most say that the children are their main or even sole responsibility. Therefore they prefer a solution that is, above all, beneficial for the children, even if it means working late hours, inconvenient shifts, and seeing less of their spouses.

> 'I used to work in a home for elderly people. I worked nearly every weekend. But then I got complaints from my children and husband, so I looked for something else. Now I work at night in a factory, so at least I have the weekends with my children and when they're asleep I start my job.'
> (Factory worker, two children, working 25 hours)

Another woman comfortably manages to combine work at a security centre with taking care of her three children but gets fed up with not seeing her spouse.

> 'I reduced my working hours, because I didn't see my husband. We both worked full continuous shifts. We communicated with each other through notes.'
> (Receptionist at an alarm centre, three children, working 20 hours)

Although most of the women in the samples have spouses, sharing tasks with their partner is not always an easy option. If women prefer a symmetric relationship they sometimes have to press to get their partner to contribute substantially to the childrearing and household tasks. It appears that women of low educational levels have fewer problems with a gender-specific division in tasks than women with more education.

'He doesn't mind that I work. As long as I can manage with my tasks at home. And he's right about that of course.'
(Receptionist, two children, working 20 hours)

Child care facilities

Although working part-time offers the best option for women to combine work and care for the children, and even if their partner contributes substantially, often other or supplementary solutions are necessary. Working part-time means having more time for (the care of) your children, but working hours do not always coincide with childrearing 'schedules.' Young children especially need to be looked after 24 hours a day, and for school age children, school hours do not necessarily coincide with working schedules.

One solution to this problem is to make use of child care facilities which are available in different forms. One such facility is playgroups for children under the age of four, where they can play two times a week for two or three hours. For women who want to work this is not a real solution. Better options for working parents are day care nurseries and after-school facilities. However, for women who had their children in the late seventies or early eighties this alternative was not available. There were very few day care centres. In 1990 a special scheme to subsidize municipal and company child care facilities was implemented resulting in the rapid growth of day nurseries and after-school facilities (Hooghiemstra & Niphuis-Nell, 1993). Although there are still long waiting lists, not all women opt for child care outside the home. Wilbrink-Griffioen (Wilbrink-Griffioen, Van Vliet & Elzinga, 1987) found that 28% of working mothers preferred a paid babysitter at home, 31% preferred an unpaid babysitter, while only 13% chose for a day care nursery. What about the working mothers in our samples?

A lot of the less educated women have an aversion to day care nurseries.

'Well I don't think that a crèche is negative, but I just didn't want it. If I was the one who wanted to have children, I should be the one who takes care of them.'
(Former administrative worker, two children)

But not all of them share this motherhood ideal.

'When she was small, it was ok. But when she was two years old I took her to the crèche, a couple of days per week, so that I could get on with my work.'
(Canine beautician who practices at home, one child, irregular hours)

Of the highly educated women who needed child care facilities only a few made or still make use of day care nurseries. One woman could take her children to a crèche at her work. The rest had or have a paid babysitter at home. The advantage of the latter, besides the household chores she often does, is that a child can stay in its own familiar surroundings and that it is easier to arrange working hours.

The highly educated women all have full-time or at least half-time jobs (20 hours per week or more), so being able to work depends mainly on a good and reliable child care arrangement.

'Well, you do hope all the time, indeed, that this babysitter, who does a good job, does not surprise you by saying I'm leaving. But basically, when the child care is okay, then the whole family is okay.'
(Secretary of an association of traders, two children, works 32 hours)

An at home babysitter is expensive. None of the highly educated women mentioned this aspect. Apparently the money is not a problem. The situation is different for women with less education. The costs of child care or a babysitter often parallel the income.

'When I was pregnant I told everybody that I was looking for an at home baby-sitter. I suc-ceeded in finding someone. She also took care of some household chores. But it was expensive. At that time I worked practically for nothing. Let's say for a period of three and a half years. Because a babysitter is very expensive. Still, I did it. I liked my job. But that's what I say: you have to be very motivated to keep working. Because you don't earn much.'
(Administration worker, one child, works 20 hours)

Because of the expense, most less educated women arrange informal kinds of child care. They ask their mothers and mothers-in-law, friends, sisters, and other mothers they know, to share in the care. The women's network in the lower classes is often more extended than that of women in the higher classes (Knijn, 1992). For less educated women with family often living next door, this is not only a practical but a socially acceptable solution.

This is less the case with highly educated women; they seem to value their independence and often don't even live close to their parents. They generally left home a while ago to study in another town and, in several cases, eventually moved due to their husbands' work. So, owing to lack of a family network and especially because they need reliable child care facilities for an extended period of time, highly educated women prefer paid babysitters. They can also afford them, because of their (much) higher household income.

Contracting out

Although the time consuming care tasks can be alleviated by child care facilities, a lot of household chores still have to be done. These can be reduced by buying time-saving household appliances or contracting out. According to Tijdens (1995), the only effective time-saving strategy is contracting out household tasks by hiring domestic help. To be able to do this, money is needed.

Highly educated women have one big advantage over other women: they have better paying jobs (partly due to the larger number of hours they work) and their spouses also have far better paid jobs than the spouses of less educated women. They can easily afford all kinds of help and facilities. With only one exception, all the families in the sample of highly educated women have domestic help for one or two mornings a week, and some hire a gardener or a window cleaner as well. For less educated women this is not the case. They themselves often hold jobs as babysitters or domestic help. There are exceptions, but most these women have rather ill paid jobs and simply can not afford this option. Their income is often thought of as supplementary to that of their spouses, and would in itself be insufficient to support the family. The next comment makes clear what money can buy.

'We just have a high income. When you accept a full-time job as a woman it means that you *must* have a high income or else you cannot afford it. Then it doesn't pay. Anyway, for care we have to pay about 1000 guilders per month and then you have your second car, going out for dinner, other holidays, more clothes. (...) We have a paid babysitter and that girl cooks, too. And we have domestic help, and someone for the garden and for the odd jobs around the house. The milkman and the greengrocer call at the house. And we have a microwave oven, a dishwasher, everything. It's a practical household.'
(Teacher at a college of higher education, 2 children, works full-time, husband is a medical specialist)

Conclusions

In this chapter, we have seen that the human capital-based explanations for differences in women's employment behaviour after the first birth still hold true even though nowadays more women of all educational levels follow this combination pattern. Although there are similarities in the strategies of the highly and less educated women, there are still differences in the boundaries that regulate and shape these strategies. Working part-time, sharing childrearing tasks with spouses, child care facilities, and contracting out the household chores are practiced by both groups of women. But there are differences in the degree to which they occur within each group.

It is still true that highly educated women are more work oriented. Combining work and childrearing is common for them. The strategies they choose are mainly directed at just staying employed, so they aim for part-time jobs without having to reduce their working hours too drastically. Furthermore, they negotiate and often bargain with their spouses for an equal division of household and childrearing tasks. Finding a reliable babysitter or child minder is another solution for these women, as well as hiring domestic help. Since they have more financial resources, these options are relatively easy to realize.

Less educated women, on the other hand, tend to be less work oriented in the sense that their work competes equally with motherhood. Most women do not see their jobs as the primary source of self-realization. Even though they often like their jobs, they prefer to spend time with their children. This preference has more to do with their opinions about being a good mother than with the supposed unattractiveness of their jobs. Therefore, the combination of work and childrearing is less obvious than it is for the highly educated women. However their behaviour is shaped by more than just their views of motherhood: these women are more restricted to an informal network of child minding. They often simply can not afford to hire a babysitter. When they can find a solution through their personal networks, they often work a few hours, on an irregular basis during school hours or on weekends and at night: whenever they can. Childrearing is their primary or sole concern: both the women themselves and their spouses share this opinion. This does not mean, however, that their spouses do not contribute to childrearing tasks or to babysitting. But as soon as a conflict arises and the combination gets more difficult, they choose for a traditional gender-specific solution, even if it means a substantial reduction in family income. Highly educated women show more enthusiasm for combining work and childrearing, but then again they have more ways to realize this option than less educated women.

One final comment we want to make is that it is imperative that empirical research on combining work and childrearing should not be considered an exclusively organisational problem. As we have seen in the life histories of the women in our sample, the women themselves have more or less room to implement the strategies they follow depending on their aspirations for childrearing and work. In an analytical sense this means we should separate the more subjective possibilities and constraints from the more objective constraints women of all educational levels face when seeking to combine work and children.

References

Hooghiemstra, B. & M. Niphuis-Nell (1993). *Sociale Atlas van de Vrouw, deel 2*. Rijswijk: SCP.
Knijn, T. (1992). Balanceren op ongelijke leggers. *Tijdschrift voor Vrouwenstudies, 13,2*, 479-509.

Ministerie van Sociale Zaken en Werkgelegenheid (1995). *Emancipatie in cijfers 1995.* Den Haag: Ministerie van Sociale Zaken en Werkgelegenheid.

Morée, M. (1992). *Mijn kinderen hebben er niets van gemerkt.* Utrecht: Jan van Arkel.

Sociaal en Cultureel Planbureau (SCP) (1994). *Sociaal en Cultureel Rapport 1994.* Rijswijk: SCP.

Tijdens, K., H. Maassen van den Brink, M. Noom & W. Groot (1994). *Arbeid en zorg.* Den Haag: OSA.

Tijdens, K. (1995). *Huishoudelijke hulp en huishoudelijke technologie.* Amsterdam: Belle van Zuylen Instituut.

Turkenburg, M. (1995). *Een baan en een kind. Aspiraties en strategieën van laagopgeleide vrouwen.* Tilburg: TUP.

Wilbrink-Griffioen, D.I., K. van Vliet & A. Elzinga (1987). *Kinderopvang en arbeidsparticipatie van vrouwen.* Den Haag: Ministerie van Sociale Zaken en Werkgelegenheid.

5
Fatherhood in transition

Suzanne Dölle
Mirjam van Dongen
Menno Jacobs

Introduction

The Western demographic life-course has undergone important changes over the last thirty years. In particular, a decline in marriage rates accompanied by a rise in divorce rates, a rise in cohabitation (without marriage) along with a rise in children born out of wedlock, and a trend towards greater equality between the rights and duties of spouses can be mentioned. These changes have different antecedents and consequences for men and women. In this chapter, we will focus on men, or, to be more precise, fathers.

Fatherhood has received special attention in recent years, in society as well as in the social sciences. The role of the father has gained in importance in society, in that it is taken more seriously. Advertising agencies use a loving and caring father as a symbol of modernity to promote all sorts of household products. Apparently the 'new father' image is capable of improving sales. The social sciences have followed these changes in society by means of a growing, though still limited, number of studies.

An important question is to what extent the new father is really participating in the daily life of the family. Men are no longer safeguarded from changes in their life pattern as a result of increased individualism, changed labour relations, and the women's movement. However, some men hang on to traditional values and norms, whereas others are willing to change their opinions and practices concerning fatherhood. This is the source of a dilemma in modern (paternal) life.

We will attempt to shed some light on the contemporary role of fatherhood by following several stages in the life-courses of men: cohabiting and childless, becoming and being a father, and fatherhood after divorce. Three different Dutch studies will be referred to in describing these stages.

The first study consists of interviews with 115 childless men and 62 fathers as a control group (Jacobs, 1994). We will consider several groups of childless men. First, we will look at men who have chosen not to have a child, at least not within the next five years. Second, we will examine men who are still in doubt as to whether they want children or not. Third, we will consider men who would welcome a child, preferably within one or two years. These will then be compared with a group of fathers.

Next, we will elaborate upon fatherhood more thoroughly, using material from interviews conducted by Van Dongen (forthcoming). Forty men were questioned about their perception and appreciation of their work and family roles. Data analysis distinguished three groups of fathers. The first and largest group consists of men who assume the role of provider, taking on hardly any child care responsibility. The second group is composed of men who are searching for a new balance between work and family life. Finally, there is a group of a few men who are highly involved in child care activities.

The last section of this chapter is devoted to divorced fathers. The results of a large nation-wide survey (Dölle, 1994) will be presented. The data were derived from a comparative study examining 'The consequences of parental changes for children' by means of a questionnaire and personal interviews with parents and adolescents in single-parent families and stepfamilies.

Choosing to become a father

Investigations on fertility, especially demographic studies, used to focus on women. The argument is straightforward and simple: It is the woman who gives birth to the child. However, it is questionable whether this one-sidedness is still justifiable. Since the 1950's, the role of the man has gained significance in making important decisions inside the home. Having children, for instance, has become a choice for both partners. The man and woman may each have their own motives, reservations, and reasons for making a positive or negative decision, as well as their unique power positions within the relationship. Also, many men and women confront a variety of conflicting interests when the issue of having children arises. These interests mostly relate to the desire for children, career ambitions, and opinions about child care. Once the first baby is born, many couples have to find a new equilibrium in the division of paid and unpaid work. And if the relationship ends in divorce or separation, the adjustment process starts all over again. This may make the decision of whether or not to become a parent a difficult one.

Ever since the role of the man in the decision-making process has increased, his responsibility for household and child care tasks has taken a different shape. Because relatively little research on fatherhood has been done, a project was started at Tilburg University. It comprises a study on the role of men in the fertility decision, their aspirations and actual participation in child care, and their father role after a divorce.

First, we will present the results of a study on the desire to become a father. 177 fecund heterosexual cohabiting Dutch men were interviewed about their motivation for parenthood, their ideas about fatherhood, their work situation, and demographical variables such as age, ethnicity, education, profession, income, and religion. These 177 men were then divided into the four groups mentioned in the introduction:

1. Those who have decided not to have a child, at least not within the next 5 years (N=22);

2. Those who have not yet decided. They are still in doubt, and cannot specify when they might want their first child (N=50);
3. Those who have decided that a child would be welcome, preferably within one or two years. Men who are part of a couple that does not use contraception belong to this category as well (N=43);
4. Those who have a child under age of two (N=62).

Motivation for parenthood

Motivation for parenthood was measured in terms of the costs and benefits of having children. This method has proven useful and is commonly applied (Hoffman & Hoffman, 1973; Van Luijn & Parent, 1990; Miller, 1994). A principal axis factor analysis on the benefits of having children indicated three categories: Affective aspects, instrumental aspects, and situational aspects. The affective aspects refer to the emotional side of becoming a father, such as giving love and affection to the child and taking care of it. The instrumental aspects refer to achieving a goal, such as enrichment of the relationship with the partner, continuing the family name, and giving meaning to life. Finally, the situational aspects refer to external factors contributing to the desire for a child, such as the opinions of family and friends, and to what Rabin (1965) calls *fatalistic* motives, such as 'it's part of life,' or a logical consequence of getting married.

The disadvantage items were also divided into three categories: Freedom-restricting aspects, responsibility aspects, and practical impediments. Restricting freedom has two elements: first, the loss of freedom in general, and second, difficulties in combining paid work or education with having children. The second category, responsibility, refers to the feeling that the responsibility of having children is too overwhelming. The third category refers to what Hoffman and Hoffman call *barriers*. Well-known barriers are a shortage of money, unsuitable housing, etc. Other 'practical impediments' are disagreement about household chores and the state of the world.

A comparison of the four groups of respondents with respect to the benefits of having children shows that all those mentioned in the questionnaire are rated lower by group 1 than by group 4. Group 2 considers eleven of the thirteen benefits less important than group 4, and group 3 also rates eleven lower than group 4. The data therefore show a constant rise in the importance of the benefits of having children along with a decrease in the time left before a positive decision is made.

The emotional aspects are considered the most important benefits of having children. 'Giving love and affection,' for example, is considered 'very important' by 34% of the men (that is, childless men and fathers), and 'important' by 54%. Instrumental benefits are seen as less important. The fact that children might be convenient in old age is considered (very) important by only 22%. Situational benefits (or 'reasons') are the least important. Almost

90% of the men disagreed with the statement 'Having children is a consequence of being married or cohabiting.'

If we look at the costs or disadvantages, we see the opposite pattern. All twelve costs are considered more important by groups 1 and 2 than by group 4, and eleven are rated higher by group 3 than by group 4. However, the freedom-restricting aspects are by far the largest problem for reluctant candidate fathers. For example, 'Having children restricts my freedom' is a statement on which 65 per cent of the childless men, and 45 per cent of the fathers, agree. Practical impediments can also be a problem. Finances and unsuitable housing are the main reasons to postpone having children. Disagreement about the division of household tasks as an impediment to having children is much less of a problem: Less than 10 per cent of the childless men and 6 per cent of the fathers consider it a problem. Responsibility is not seen as an important cost. One out of ten men do not disagree with the statement, 'I cannot handle the responsibility.' The difference between childless men and fathers is small in this respect.

In short, these data seem to indicate that it is not so much a rise in benefits that facilitates a positive decision, but the diminishing of the perceived costs of having children that paves the way to fatherhood.

Ideas about fatherhood
It is safe to assume that men begin thinking about their own role as a father as soon as they start to think about having children, i.e., as soon as they develop a motivation for parenthood. Still, more than 45 per cent of the men who did not want children within the next five years claim to have (very) clear ideas about their fatherhood roles. When the time frame becomes shorter, the picture becomes clear to even more men. However, approximately 30 per cent of the fathers claim not to know exactly what fatherhood means to them. The aspect mentioned by the majority of men is raising the child. Next (in descending order of frequency) are responsibility, income, taking care of the child or giving love and affection, being a family, and being a friend to the child. We see that the more emotional aspects of being a father (such as taking care of the child, being a family) are mentioned least. Many men see 'responsible' tasks, such as nurturing and providing an income, as the most important aspects of their father role. If our assumption is right, namely that men really begin thinking about their own role as a father after they have developed a motivation for parenthood, it might be plausible to assume that the traditional picture that emerges from these figures is a result of the unconsciously internalised ideas about fatherhood of their own fathers.

Another remarkable thing about these notions of fatherhood is the discrepancy between ideal and everyday life. Many men (over 60%) mention the fact that they would like to work fewer hours per week once they have children. In fact, if we compare childless men with fathers, we see that, on average, fathers work even more hours per week.

The work situation

Having a paid job can be a big obstacle to having children. If husband and wife both have full-time jobs, having children is even less likely to be a topic of serious consideration. This is not to say that it is not a matter for discussion or argument. In most cases, it is eventually the woman who cuts back on work when the first baby is about to be born.

The men in this study were asked to evaluate their employer on a few aspects concerning the combination of having a job and a child. However, many men seemed ill-informed about their legal rights. A quarter of those interviewed answered the question 'Do you think your employer would be willing to give you parental leave if you asked for it?' with 'Don't know,' whereas parental leave is a legal right in the Netherlands. Another twenty per cent think that it would be very difficult, if not impossible, to get parental leave. Only about thirty per cent think part-time work would be possible.

Socio-economic status

Many authors have argued that high socio-economic status has a positive effect on fertility (Lewis, Newson & Newson, 1982; Beckman, 1983; Hollerbach, 1983; Seccombe, 1991). Unfortunately, our sample was too small to reject or support this hypothesis. However, it may be partially rejected on theoretical grounds. Socio-economic status is often operationalized as a function of education, profession, and income. These things tend to rise as one gets older. This means that socio-economic status is, at least partly, determined by age. No one will deny the effect of age on fertility, so the correlation between socio-economic status and fertility might be spurious, caused by the correlation between socio-economic status and age.

Becoming a father is not something that 'just happens,' although it may have been 'a part of life' for many years. Only 5 per cent of the men (father or not) feel that having children is inextricably linked with marriage or a steady relationship. Seventeen per cent of the childless men and 21 per cent of the fathers feel it is a part of life. Sixty per cent of the couples frequently talk about whether or not they want children.

Becoming a father has become a difficult decision for many men. This is not to say that the choice for women is any easier. Still, most couples come to a positive decision sooner or later. However, as we have seen, many men promise more than they can actually deliver. They say they would like to work fewer hours per week, but end up working even more hours after the child is born. How do their ideals, or aspirations, relate to real life? What are their ideas about fatherhood with regard to work and a career immediately after they have their first child? In the next section we will elaborate upon these questions.

Aspirations and practices of fatherhood

The new ideal encourages paternal involvement, but there is no single model for them to follow. It is therefore important to acknowledge that in our pluralistic Western society, various interpretations of the father role coexist. Fathers fill many roles which vary in relative importance from one context to another. A man's main legitimisation for being the primary economic provider has to do with socio-economic circumstances and opportunities, and with conventions about the male gender identity. The economic sphere continues to offer insufficient opportunities to men and women alike to reconcile work and family life. Although men shape their own fatherhood practices, they do not do so in circumstances of their own choosing. This section is based on a study by Van Dongen (forthcoming), derived from interviews with 40 randomly (although not representatively) selected men with children under the age of five. The fathers interviewed live rather traditionally and mostly have full-time employment.

The concept of fatherhood is in a transition phase, having undergone several changes in attitudes, experiences, and perspectives (Van Dongen, Frinking & Jacobs, 1995). As a result of sweeping cultural, economic, and demographic changes, many men ask themselves what it means to be a father in modern society and they start to rethink the fatherhood role. While the last generation experienced its aspirations and practices as natural and reasonable, the younger generation might judge these as unthinkable and exasperating. Even though the old meanings of fatherhood may be questioned, they have not been fully replaced by new ones. The younger generation may experience a discrepancy between the manners, values, and ideals of the older generation, and those which prevail in our society today. Past experiences are, however, part of men's habitus and old and new ideals form a part of the younger generation's aspirations and practices. Thus, while men may try to challenge the old meanings of fatherhood, they may justify the self-evidence of those meanings as well.

Times have changed. Pressure is increasing for men to participate more actively in home life. At a general level, Dutch men show an awareness of new rules that prescribe equal rights and duties for men and women concerning work and family roles. Many of them agree that they are just as responsible as their partner for performing household and child care tasks. Many men think those tasks should be equally divided between the couple. A large majority do not consider their role as economic provider their most important task. They judge their own child rearing skills equal to those of the mother. It is important, however, to draw a line between what is judged acceptable for members of a society at large and personal preferences of an individual for his own life.

The personal preferences of those interviewed suggest a desire for close involvement with their children. At a personal level, for some men this entails becoming their children's playmates and regular or irregular babysitters. Other men may enjoy participating in daily caretaking and sharing parental responsibilities. Three types of fathers are distinguished, based on the aspirations and practices of the men surveyed: providers, co-providers and care takers.

Providers
Despite the labour force participation of the female partner, the majority of men involved in this study fulfilled the provider role. For these *providers*, being a father implies a direct relationship with the children, but does not necessarily mean they are eager to take care for them on a daily basis. They take their partner's active involvement in the early stages of the child's life for granted. These men nevertheless veer away from the traditional role of the economic provider. Filling the father role in this way may cause them to become an outsider who brings home the paycheck but otherwise has little connection with his children. These men's perception of fatherhood therefore also includes some family involvement. They perceive providing economic support alongside family involvement as reasonable and common-sense behaviour, not only because they are possible, but also because these behaviours are most likely to be positively sanctioned. The dilemma these men face is how to sustain a belief in active father involvement added to successful providing, in the light of the new ideal of fatherhood and the limited amount of time they have available for their children compared to their partners.

For most of these men, coming home in the evening coincides with the end of the children's day. This is problematic, since it means that their contribution to direct child rearing activities is not consistent with the ideal of active father involvement. Consequently, they feel they should somehow compensate at a practical level for their absence during the day. It is the generalised involvement of the man in all aspects of caring for the children, expressed in his desire to assume some child care responsibility in order to support his partner in her interests outside the home, that is felt to prove his involvement.

In some families, the woman's earnings make up an important part of the total family income and are often perceived as a financial necessity. Some of these provider men, however, earmark their partner's earnings for extra expenses. Limiting the uses of the partner's income to get 'something extra' helps maintain the definition of the man as the primary provider and the woman as an additional contributor who can quit working any time she wants. This definition of the female work role prevents men giving up (some of) the privileges they have as economic providers and allows them to assign domestic tasks and responsibilities to their partners. To alleviate any disruption of gender equality, these men tend to legitimise the larger contributions of the mother by emphasising the importance of their wives' physical presence, in that the child may suffer if their mother is not around enough.

These men are thus confronted with a contradiction in their beliefs in the fairness of active father involvement and gender equality on the one hand, and the current family organisation on the other. Some men believe that a father should be directly involved, but in practice, support traditional family patterns.

Co-providers

The second group consists of *co-providers*. This group of fathers endorses the principles that prescribe the equal rights and duties of men and women and does not conform to traditional norms of the complementary family. These men face a dilemma, in that institutionalised support for combining work and child rearing is not sufficient, and they have difficulty accepting the orthodox male role as the economic provider.

Given the difficult choice between active family involvement and less opportunity for career-building on the one hand, and the unattractive alternative of sole economic provider on the other, some men avoid (confronting) the question of how to integrate an active involvement in child rearing into lives geared to work. Cumulative experience in the economic sphere appears to make a definite choice in favour of active involvement in child care increasingly difficult. However, traditional division of labour patterns may take over later on, if they were to follow common patterns of behaviour in the beginning of their fatherhood. Since these men perceive an active participation in child rearing as both rewarding and costly, approach and avoidance describe their demeanour. This ambivalence leads to choosing different options at different times to deal with the dilemma of how to reconcile work and family roles.

For some co-providers, the decision to be actively engaged in child rearing involves assessing the possibilities and impossibilities of holding onto a satisfying job and weighing these alternatives against each other. Most men who opt for active and direct involvement, do not consider significantly reducing their workload an acceptable alternative. They believe it would jeopardise their financial position. Although a perspective that views active involvement of the father as conditional ignores the difficulties caused by combining work and family, it also reflects the uncertainties men experience. Fathers may find themselves in a state of 'perplexed bewilderment' due to the contradictions of 'emergent fatherhood' (Lewis, 1986). Recognizing the existence of different beliefs does not automatically generate preferences for one's own life. Other co-providers plan to become actively involved as a father. These men advance the notion of sharing because of a sense of commitment towards the child's upbringing and their wives' professional pursuits. Their view is supported by the statement that 'a child has two parents, not one.'

Knowing other actively engaged fathers directly and substantially affects the perceived costs and benefits of highly involved fatherhood versus economic providing, since it causes a recognition of choices made possible by competing or even antagonistic beliefs. These men are willing to compromise in order to meet their own desire for emotional satisfaction. A commitment to a non-domestic woman can also affect the perceived costs and benefits of child rearing and providing.

For some co-providers involved fatherhood and commitment to their wives are closely linked. They accept, even appreciate, the fact that their partners place non-domestic pursuits on a par with domestic ones and, as a result, these men think that it is only fair if their work commitments are compatible with hers. These men refer to the so-called 'motherhood dilemma.' They try to lighten the burden of child rearing for women by starting their own business or by choosing work patterns that make family commitments and work obligations easier to balance.

All co-providers conclude that their careers may suffer as a result of active involvement in child rearing, but that the costs of a nurturing father role can be kept within acceptable limits. Moreover, the costs of sole economic providing might be unmanageable. Active involvement in child care is considered a good thing to do. Co-providers look for a new balance between the relative importance of work and family roles.

Care takers
A few men mentioned active parenting as the central component of their fatherhood aspirations and practices. These *care takers* blend traditional paternal and maternal roles. They join with mothers as equal partners in child care activities. A strong work commitment on the part of women may lead to practices that many men perceive as improbable or even unthinkable. Only a few fathers actually admitted that during the transition to parenthood, the idea of being at home with the children all day appealed to them. It is rare for a couple to switch parenting and work duties completely, but a non-domestic partner with a strong desire for children and a belief that it is better for a child if one of the parents is physically present during the day, may cause a father to become the care taker. For these men the partner's desire for professional achievement appears to trigger highly involved fathering.

The care takers are convinced that fathers are as capable of raising children as the mothers. In fact, they compete with mothers in terms of the skills required for raising and caring for children. In accordance with the principles of regulation that prescribe gender equality, men are given the same nurturing abilities as women. In their opinion, the nurturing aptitude that used to be reserved for women has lost its validity. These fathers see men and women as interchangeable when it comes to parenting.

The accounts of these care takers suggest that theories that portray men as universally uninterested in children and uniformly underdeveloped in their nurturing needs and desires oversimplify men's orientations toward parenting. The motivations for active father involvement of these two types of men go beyond the desire to reproduce offspring merely to prove their manhood or to perpetuate the family name. On the contrary, these men possess a genuine desire to nurture children. For care takers, changing principles have become the unifying force in their fatherhood practices. For these men, the role of the nurturing father does not belong to the field of heterodoxic beliefs, but is seen as a logical thing to do.

The overall picture of fatherhood aspirations and practices is one of resistance and change. Contemporary fathers are confronted with rules that encourage men to take part in child rearing activities. But new styles of fathering have failed to completely eliminate the male provider role. Since common culture has a hold on men, cultural messages about the male's role in the family discourage too much open deviation. Equivalence, thus, often prevails over equality.

Fathers seem to face a dilemma between affectionate concern for their children and successful breadwinning. Attitudes are moving in the direction of more love and care; practice is lagging behind. It is essential to recognize, however, that the impetus toward new paternal activity has been seriously counterbalanced by a rise in the divorce rate. How do men fulfil their paternal role after the family has broken up?

Fatherhood after divorce

This section aims to present a picture of the changes in fatherhood and paternal participation after divorce. Do fathers try to maintain close bonds following a divorce and stay involved in the lives of their children, as a 'closely involved' father? Or do they gradually drift away from their children, losing contact, becoming a 'distant' or 'lost' father.

The number of divorces in the Netherlands has shot up in the past decades, more or less stabilising in recent years. About one in three marriages ends in divorce. One in every five children is confronted with their parents' divorce while still a minor. These children grow up in single-parent families for at least part of their childhoods. The number of single-parent families in the Netherlands has grown considerably in recent years.

Though there is a growing scientific interest in divorce and how it affects children, the role of the non-custodial parent has received very little attention from scholars. Those studies which have addressed the subject, both in the Netherlands and elsewhere, shed very little light on the involvement of the father after divorce.

Joint custody after divorce is not always an option. The judge decides which of the parents will be awarded custody of the minor children. Even under the more gender-neutral custody laws that more and more courts have adopted, in the vast majority of recent divorce cases custody has been awarded to the mother (Van Wamelen, 1987; Wegelin, 1990). Continuing paternal participation and a close involvement with the children after divorce is not always easy to realize. In their new position, fathers are faced with many legal, emotional, social, and financial problems.

In order to gain more insight into fatherhood after divorce, we made use of data derived from a project composed of a quantitative and a qualitative phase. In the first phase (1991), a written survey was held among a representative national sample of 1596 families, with children between 12 and 17 years old. Three types of families were distinguished: nuclear families, single-parent families and stepfamilies. The second phase of the study (1993) included a qualitative follow-up survey during which these adolescents and their parents were interviewed yielding a total of 180 personal interviews for the three types of families.

Changes in the paternal role after divorce

Changes in the paternal role after divorce can best be understood by referring to the role of fathers in the intact nuclear family. Resident fathers participate in child rearing directly by disciplining their children, exercising authority, teaching values, giving affection, caring for their physical needs, and serving as role models. Fathers participate in parenting indirectly by providing economic support to the family (breadwinner) and by sharing household chores. After a break-up the parents no longer share the responsibilities of child care. Post-divorce fatherhood incorporates a variety of new tasks and responsibilities. Three responsibilities define the role of the non-resident father: participation in child rearing decisions (how to raise the children), social involvement (spending time with the children), and economic involvement (paying alimony or child support) (Seltzer & Bianchi, 1988; Seltzer, 1991).

The first dimension which is distinguished is *participation in child rearing decisions*. After divorce, the non-resident father is no longer closely involved in the daily routine of family life. The father's influence on the major decisions in the children's lives will diminish when living apart. The children's development can only be followed at a distance.

With regard to the second dimension, *social involvement*, the amount of time fathers spend with their children is limited after divorce. The former spouses usually make visiting arrangements. Not only the frequency of contact but also the quality and intensity of contact changes (reduces) over time.

The third element of a father's involvement concerns the *economic ties* which are maintained after divorce. After a break-up, fathers are faced with rigorous child support obligations. Depending on their income and circumstances, the amount of the child support (alimony) is fixed. Living apart from the children, fathers face less stringent requirements and stimuli to provide for the children's material needs. Thus, the motivation to contribute to child support may decline rapidly.

How do non-resident fathers cope with the changes in fatherhood after divorce? Non-resident fathers vary widely in the degree to which they fulfil their role responsibilities. In the early period after divorce they usually explore the different strategies of fathering. Over time a more stable definition of the non-resident father role is established. A minority of fathers remain involved in all three dimensions of the paternal role ('involved fathers'); most fathers fulfil two roles ('visiting fathers') and the rest are involved in one or none of the aspects of child care after divorce ('distant fathers'). Since the three (behaviourial) dimensions of paternal involvement are closely related (positively associated), they are discussed together with the three types of non-resident fathers.

Involved fathers
A minority of fathers (about 10%) maintain close bonds with their children after a divorce (Dölle, 1993). Although living apart, they stay closely involved in the children's lives and continue to influence their development. By participating in as many child rearing activities as possible (nurturing, supervising, supporting, and decision-making) they try to compensate for their (physical) absence in the family. In a few cases, the parental responsibilities are equally divided between the former spouses after divorce. Both parents share child rearing activities and decision-making about important aspects of the children's lives, such as education and health care, for example, helping the children decide which school to go to. The children are completely incorporated in the father's new household where they frequently stay over; sometimes co-residence is set up. During the extended visits, fathers have practical responsibility for the children in providing for their physical and emotional needs: preparing meals, buying clothes, comforting and supporting them. A close and equal relationship with mutual understanding between father and child is established. The involved fathers feel a responsibility to provide the material needs of the children. Consequently, contributing to the children's economic support, in order to guarantee or improve their material well-being, is a self-evident commitment. Overall these fathers take an active role in all dimensions of child care after divorce. They are particularly child-oriented and motivated to participate in their upbringing. The fathers' close involvement in most cases is a logical continuation of the pre-divorce situation, where they shared the responsibility of raising the children. The positive association between the three components of divorced fatherhood persists over time.

Visiting fathers
Most fathers (about two-thirds) establish a new visiting relationship with their children after divorce (Dölle, 1994). The once-in-a-fortnight arrangement is the most common. Children who frequently visit their fathers have face-to-face-interaction as well as telephone or mail contact. As the children get older, the frequency of contact diminishes. Regular visits provide an opportunity for parents to see each other and discuss the children or plan the next visit. Although some fathers continue to discuss the children with their former spouse, they don't have much influence on major child rearing decisions (13%). In a majority of

cases, however, parents have little contact with each other. These fathers retain some indirect influence over their children. Over time, most of the visiting fathers get used to their new roles. Some rediscover the importance of fatherhood for the development and welfare of the children, who seem to appreciate their father's attention and emotional involvement more than the material aspects of the contact, such as presents and trips.

Alternatively, some of the non-resident fathers develop a superficial relationship, based only on material needs. They organise recreational activities for the weekends to entertain their children, buying them presents and toys, or taking them to amusement parks to avoid delicate questions about the divorce. The father's contribution to the economic welfare of the children depends on the frequency of contact. Fathers who spend a lot of time with their children are not only more likely to make regular child support payments to the mother but tend to make more supplementary contributions. Visiting and paying child support basically defines a father's relationship to his children. Two-thirds of the fathers continue to be involved and maintain primarily social and economic ties. On the other hand, they exercise little authority over decisions that affect the children's lives. Their involvement with their children is likely to diminish over time. As the frequency of contact decreases, the economic investments and participation in decisions diminishes.

Distant fathers
Over time, fathers and children often lose touch with each other (about 30%). Some fathers withdraw completely from their post-divorce roles. One-quarter of all children in single-parent families have lost contact with the non-custodial parent (Van Gelder, 1987; Dölle, 1993). For various reasons, involvement in the three dimensions of paternity declines after divorce. Some fathers share the opinion that fatherhood demands a full commitment to the role. Since they live apart from the children, fulfilling their paternal responsibilities has become rather difficult. In the belief that it's-all-or-nothing they slowly withdraw.

Other fathers consider the costs of part-time fatherhood too high and sever the bonds with their children who no longer fit into their new lives and different living arrangements. Other fathers limit contact with their children because of fear of failure and disappointment. They are afraid of not being able to live up to the expectations or meet the needs of their children. Managing their distress, answering their questions, supporting them emotionally, requires energy and experience which they lack. They are disappointed in themselves for failing to solve their children's problems. Consequently, they limit or avoid further contact.

Some fathers feel guilty about breaking up the family. Regular contact with the children would intensify their guilt or they haven't yet learned to cope with the pain of the divorce. Seeing the children reminds them of this stressful and painful event. Others reduce contact in order to avoid any confrontation with their former spouse. As a result, these non-resident fathers gradually drift away from their children. Some remarry, establish a new family, move far away, find new employment and leisure activities (50% of all divorced men: CBS, 1990). These new commitments and constraints compete with the children for their father's time, attention, and money. Prior to divorce these fathers were not actively involved in household chores and child care tasks. Their main function was as breadwinner. Developing a new style of fatherhood after divorce is rather difficult. After exploring alternate strategies of fathering they subsequently withdraw from their roles. Initially the father's involvement is sporadic, but over the course of time their involvement declines rapidly. Their paternal role is mainly defined by paying obligatory child support. Contact with the children is limited and their decision-making influence diminishes in most cases.

Factors related to long-term involvement

How successfully fathers fulfil their new roles appears to be related to several factors: the division of responsibilities prior to divorce, the attitude of the mother, elapsed time since the divorce, and uncertainty about the father's role:

The role of the father in raising the children depends on the division of responsibilities prior to divorce. Fathers who were actively involved with their children during the marriage maintain this involvement after divorce. Those who hardly shared any child rearing activities in the nuclear family show less paternal involvement after divorce. The father's involvement with the children after divorce also depends on the extent to which mothers allow their former spouses to participate in making child rearing decisions. Resident mothers often reject any participation of the father. Only in a minority of cases do fathers share in the decision-making about important aspects of their children's live. The mothers who are willing to accept the father's contribution used to share child care tasks during marriage. Most fathers, however, have little say in the decision-making process after divorce. The amount of time spent living apart from the children is related to the father's involvement. The frequency of contact and the influence on the children usually decline after at least three years. Conflicting and ambiguous expectations about the paternal role after divorce in our society accounts for confusion and uncertainty. An absence of clear rules or norms for non-resident fathers complicates the issue. A lack of clarity about what specific behaviour is appropriate towards the children causes doubt. Ambiguity concerning the responsibilities of non-resident fathers towards their children hampers the smooth transition to their new roles.

The future of post-divorce fatherhood

Over the past couple of decades, joint custody legislation has gradually been adopted and the participation of the father in child rearing activities has slowly increased. Despite these changes, mothers still bear primary responsibility for raising children after a divorce. A father's involvement in his children's lives diminishes over the course of the divorce, with the non-resident father often becoming nothing more than a spectator.

Given the high divorce rates and rapid changes in the division of parental tasks and responsibilities during marriage, changes in post-divorce fatherhood are bound to take place. Fathers who are closely involved with their children during marriage try to maintain this involvement after divorce. The extent of pre-divorce involvement may affect how engaged a post-divorce father will be: a growing number of divorced fathers may attempt to arrange joint custody (or co-parenting) for the children.

These developments would ameliorate the negative effects of parental changes on children. Since scholars focus on the importance of participation of the non-resident parent for the well-being of the children after divorce, a continuing, stable, and close relationship with the non-resident parent (father) appears to be related to successful long-term adjustment to the parental changes. Frequent (if good) contact is generally favourable since the child manages to adjust to and cope with the changes in the family situation (Jacobson, 1978; Hess & Camara, 1979; Rosen, 1979; Gongla & Thompson, 1987; Van Gelder, 1989). Encouraging the non-resident father to stay involved in the three dimensions of fatherhood could improve the children's well-being after divorce.

Conclusion

Becoming a parent is more than just the decision to have a child. It entails, for example, specifying one's ideas of parenthood. These specifications differ for men and women. In this chapter we focused on men. It is not clear whether men realize the sorts of conflicts they may encounter once they have decided in favour of parenthood. A decrease in the perception of disadvantages just before the first child is born does not necessarily mean that this picture prevails. Problems may arise at a later time. However, if all the possible problems that a birth might cause are identified, the positive aspects may be overlooked, and few children would ever be born. Considering every aspect of the choice to have children - which is impossible - would make it an awful dilemma. Some men realize this, and for them it is a dilemma. The majority of men do not seem too bothered by it.

The second dilemma of fatherhood deals with the decline in cultural support for the male as economic provider and the increasing pressure for more father involvement. Since many men still function as the (main) provider, they face the dilemma of how to alleviate any disruption of the idea of active family involvement. To be more actively engaged with their children, men need to reduce or restructure their role as workers. Here, we encounter a conflict of old and new norms.

The third dilemma arises after a divorce. Once again the father has to make a decision about his involvement with his children. Will he be an involved, a visiting, or a distant father? Perhaps his notion of fatherhood will persist after a divorce. Or perhaps his ideas will change, which is, after all, not very unlikely, since his role as a father changes after a divorce. Cross-sectional surveys shed light on the separate life-course stages, but very little is known about the coherence of these pre- and post-transitional periods.

In order to know more about the whole range of options, problems, and solutions with regard to fatherhood, it is of great importance to study the issue from a life-course perspective. Every choice and dilemma can only be understood in terms of other choices and dilemmas and their outcomes.

References

Beckman, L.J. (1983). Communication, power, and the influence of social networks in couple decisions on fertility. In R.A. Bulatao & R.D. Lee (Eds.), *Determinants of fertility in developing countries*. New York: Academic Press.

Centraal Bureau voor de Statistiek (CBS) (1990). *Onderzoek Gezinsvorming 1988. Samenwonen, trouwen, geboorteregeling, werken en kinderen krijgen*. Den Haag: SDU.

Dölle, S.P.M. (1993). *Kinderen na echtscheiding en hertrouw*. Tilburg: Tilburg University Press.

Dölle, S.P.M. (1994). *Opgroeien in een één-ouder- of stiefgezin*. Tilburg: Tilburg University Press.

Dongen, M.C.P. van, G.A.B. Frinking & M.J.G. Jacobs (1995). *Changing Fatherhood: an interdisciplinary perspective*. Amsterdam: Thesis Publishers.

Dongen, M. van (forthcoming). *Aspirations and practices of fatherhood*.

Gelder, K. van (1987). *Alleen zorgen: Een onderzoek naar het functioneren van een-oudergezinnen*. Den Haag: NIMAWO.

Gelder, K. van (1989). *Kinderen van de rekening? Een-ouder-kinderen in de onderzoeks-literatuur*. Den Haag: NIMAWO.

Gongla, P.A. & E.H. Thompson (1987). Single Parent Families. In Sussman & Steinmetz (Eds.), *Handbook of Marriage and the Family*. pp. 397-418.

Hess, R.D. & K.A. Camara (1979). Post-Divorce Family Relationships as Mediating Factors in the Consequences of Divorce for Children. *Journal of Social Issues*, 79-96.

Hoffman, L.W. & M.L. Hoffman (1973). The value of children to parents. In J.T. Fawcett (Ed.), *Psychological perspectives on population*. pp. 1-76. New York: Basic Books.

Hollerbach, P.E. (1983). Fertility decision-making processes: A critical essay. In R.A. Bulatao & R.D. Lee (Eds.), *Determinants of fertility in developing countries*. New York: Academic Press.

Jacobs, M.J.G. (1994). *The wish to become a father: How do men decide?* Paper prepared for the conference on Changing Fatherhood, WORC, Tilburg University.

Jacobson, D.S. (1978). The Impact of Marital Separation/Divorce on Children. *Journal of divorce. Vol I & II.*

Lewis, C. (1986). *Becoming a father*. Milton Keynes: Open University Press.

Lewis, C., J. Newson & E. Newson (1982). Father participation through childhood and its relation to career aspirations and delinquency. In N. Beail & J. McGuire (Eds.), *Fathers: Psychological perspectives*. London: Junction.

Luijn, H. van & A. Parent (1990). *Laatste kans-moeders. Een onderzoek naar vrouwen die twijfelen over het krijgen van kinderen.* NISSO-studies nr. 8, Delft.

Miller W.B. (1994). Childbearing motivations, desires and intentions: A theoretical framework. *Genetic, Social and General Psychology Monographs, 120(2)*, 223-258.

Rabin, A.I. (1965). Motivation for parenthood. *Journal of Projective Techniques and Personality Assessment, 29*, 405-411.

Rosen, R. (1979). Some critical issues concerning children of divorce. *Journal of Divorce*, 19-25.

Seccombe, K. (1991). Assessing the costs and benefits of children: Gender comparisons among childfree husbands and wives. *Journal of Marriage and the Family, 53*, 191-202.

Seltzer, J. & S.M. Bianchi (1988). Children's Contact with Absent Parents. *Journal of Marriage and the Family, 50*, 663-677.

Seltzer, J. (1991). Relationships between Fathers and Children who Live Apart. *Journal of Marriage and the Family, 53*, 79-101.

Wamelen, C. van (1987). *Ouderschap en ouderlijk gezag na scheiding*. Zwolle.

Wegelin, M. (1990). *Moeders en vaders, scheiden en delen; constructies van gelijkheid in de verdeling van het ouderschap na echtscheiding*. Amsterdam.

6

Dilemma or compromise:
The division of housework and child care among dual earners

Hester van der Vinne
Mascha Brink

Introduction

In this chapter, the focus will be on the division of housework and child care between men and women in families. The central issue will be the often observed gap between attitudes concerning the division of this unpaid labour and the actual division of work. Despite the fact that a large majority of Dutch people favour an equal division of housework and child care between men and women, numerous studies have shown, and continue to show that the actual division is far from equal. This finding raises several questions of both practical and more theoretical relevance. The first question concerns the correspondence between attitudes and behaviour: what is the relationship between the two? In the case of the division of housework and child care in the Netherlands, where many advocate an equal division but few practice it, this relationship seems to be weak, to say the least. How do men and women experience the relationship between their opinions and actions? Do they acknowledge that there is a gap between their beliefs and actions? Is this gap a dilemma? Does it bother them? When they explain their division of labour, do they attempt to close the gap and if so, how? We hope to answer some of these questions. We will first give a short overview of the actual division of housework and attitudes concerning the division of labour between men and women. In particular, studies linking the two will be discussed. We will then make an inventory of explanations that have been given to account for the possible differences between attitudes and behaviour. Finally, the plausibility of these explanations will be assessed, using data from a (largely qualitative) study in which 25 couples talked about the division of tasks in their household, how and why it came about, and how and why it is maintained.

Theoretical viewpoints

In recent years, the division of labour in families has become a popular subject of scientific research in the Netherlands as elsewhere. Many researchers have tried to explain the phenomenon. The three theories most frequently used in the social sciences are new home economics, exchange theory, and role theory (Van der Lippe, 1993).

In new home economics, the reasoning is as follows. Individuals have knowledge and skills at their disposal: their human capital. Like financial capital, they try to use this human capital in the most profitable way. In dividing their time between paid and unpaid labour, men and women let their amount of human capital, expressed as their potential value in the labour market, guide their choices. If their potential earning power is greater, their time is more valuable and therefore their participation in unpaid labour is more expensive. The household is seen as a unit that tries to maximize its outcomes by dividing paid and unpaid work in the most profitable way. Accordingly, the person with the highest earning power in the labour market will work more hours outside the home and the person with the lower earning power will do more housework. From our point of view, this theory has several drawbacks. It assumes, for instance, that people base their choices exclusively on issues of time and money, and does not take institutional restrictions or social norms into account. A more important drawback, however, is the assumption of maximizing the outcome, for this assumption renders the question *why* labour is divided in a certain way irrelevant: labour is distributed in a particular way because it is most profitable for both partners in the household.

In contrast, exchange theory does not see the family as one unit trying to maximize a joint outcome, but instead focuses on differences in resources between partners. It states that in an interaction each will try to minimize her or his costs in order to achieve the best possible outcome for her- or himself. To obtain this outcome, people use their resources, most of them socio-economic, such as education, occupational status, and income. An exchange relationship will exist as long as all parties profit from the exchange. In terms of the division of labour, this means that each of the two partners will try to divide the labour according to her or his preference. The decision about the division of tasks then, is based on the relative resources of each partner. In this model, the partner with the most resources will have more power in the relationship and will do less housework than the partner with less resources. A limitation of this theory is the assumption that housework is something both partners will try to avoid whenever possible. It does not leave any room for people who actually like housework and child care. In addition, exchange theory (like new home economics) does not incorporate institutional limitations and social norms regarding the division of labour between men and women.

Both new home economics and exchange theory see structural factors as determinants of the division of paid and unpaid work in families. Both theories assume that there is some kind of balance between paid and unpaid work: there is a fixed amount of work to be done and if one partner does the paid work, the other will have to do the unpaid work. Or, if both partners have paid work, they will have to share the unpaid work as well. As a result, these theories are less suited to explain inequality in families where both partners work outside the home.

According to the third theory, role theory, women and men are taught from a young age how to behave, i.e., what their appropriate roles should be. These (often gender-specific) role expectations are then internalized to shape gender role attitudes. Role theory applied to the division of labour in families means that this division is influenced by gender role attitudes. It is hypothesized that egalitarian attitudes towards capacities and roles of women and men go together with a more equal division of labour in the home, and non-egalitarian attitudes with a traditional division of labour (the man as provider and the woman as housewife). This theory is especially interesting for policymakers who hope to change the division of labour by changing people's attitudes. However, we have seen in Chapter 1 that if we take the Dutch population as a whole, the widely shared egalitarian gender role attitudes go together with a decidedly unequal division of labour between women and men. Whether or not this apparent inconsistency also occurs at the individual level and how people deal with it will be discussed in detail later on.

First, the developments in the division of unpaid labour in the Netherlands will be described. For the purposes of this chapter, we define unpaid labour as housework and child care. These two taken together will be referred to as family work, encompassing all activities required to support a family. We realize that this definition excludes other forms of unpaid labour, e.g., volunteer work, caring for the elderly (these are, for the most part, performed by women), but since no other form of unpaid labour consumes as much of a woman's time as her family, we consider this to be the main form. How, then, are housework and child care divided in the Netherlands, and has this division changed as dramatically as the distribution of paid labour?

The division of housework and child care between men and women in the Netherlands
For a long time, policymakers in the Netherlands have ignored the area of unpaid labour. The focus of equal opportunity policies has been on women's participation in paid labour, for which they appear to have been quite successful. Women's participation in the labour force has increased substantially over the last decades. The issue of unpaid labour, although it had been recognized by feminists as far back as the late 1960s as an inhibitor of female employment (Smit, 1967), did not appear in equal opportunity policies until 1993, when 'the redistribution of unpaid labour,' and more specifically, increasing men's share in unpaid labour, was named as one of the three spearheads of Dutch emancipation policy (Tweede Kamer, 1992/1993), along with increasing women's share in political and societal decision making and breaking through stereotypical images of masculinity and feminity. The redistribution of unpaid labour is regarded as a way to stimulate female participation in the labour force, which, in its turn, is seen as a way for women to achieve economic self-sufficiency. The issue of unpaid labour has been changed from a private matter, to be negotiated between men and women in their own homes, to an official target of government policy.

In 1990 72% of family work in the Netherlands was performed by women, compared to 78% in 1975. Women now spend 30.7 hours per week on family work (see also Table

Dilemma or compromise

6.1), which means a decrease of 3 hours over the last 20 years. Men spend 14.6 hours per week on family work - an increase of 2.2 hours over the same period (SCP, 1994a). In general, it can be said that women's share in family work has decreased somewhat in recent years.

Table 6.1: Time spent on family work in the Netherlands in hours per week

	Women	Men
By Age of Children		
No Children	31.0	17.8
Children < 6	51.6	20.2
Children 6 - 14	39.9	13.3
Children > 14	39.5	14.1
TOTAL	30.7	14.6

It has often been demonstrated, however, that the division of labour in a family is influenced strongly by the presence of (small) children (De Jong & De Olde, 1994). Van der Lippe and Niphuis-Nell (1994) have calculated the differences in men's and women's time allocation between 1975 and 1990, taking into account the number and age of children in the household. If households with and without children are examined separately, we see that in households without children, women now spend considerably less time on housework than they did in 1975 - a decrease of 5.7 hours. Their spouses have increased their number of hours spent on housework slightly (2.8 hours more than in 1975). So time spent on housework by men and women who share a household without children has equalized somewhat. Different patterns emerge in households with children. Women with children over 5 years of age have decreased their time spent on housework and child care by 3.9 or by 3.0 hours (women with children over 14).

Women with small children under the age of 5, however, spent more time on family work in 1990 than they did in 1975, an increase of 2 hours. The fathers of these children under 5 have also increased their time spent on family work, by 4.5 hours. The contribution of fathers with children over 5 years of age has hardly changed over those 15 years; their contribution remains around 13 hours per week. Women without children spend less time on housework than ever, and more time is spent on small children.

The statistics mentioned above were calculated for working women and housewives combined. Therefore, they do not take into account another important difference between women: the number of hours they spend on paid work. As can be gathered from the number of women in part-time jobs, women differ greatly (much more than men) in the number of hours they spend on paid work. If women are grouped according to their participation in full-time employment, and unemployment, we see that the hours worked outside the home have a strong influence on the hours spent on family work, as was demonstrated in Chapter 1 (Table 1.5). The difference between married women without a job and women with a full-time job is substantial, whereas for men this difference does not exist. However, as mentioned earlier, the largest group of working women in the Netherlands consists of those with part-time jobs. These women still spend 33.6 hours a week on family work while their husbands contribute even less than the husbands of the housewives. These women have opted for part-time work because they want some time for their domestic responsibilities, but this strategy backfires: they often have a longer work week (paid and unpaid labour combined) than their spouse, a housewife, and longer even than women with full-time jobs. Even though it seems that, in general, inequalities between men and women are diminishing, there is a large group of women for whom this is not true at all.

Gender role attitudes and the division of family work

If gender role attitudes really were to have a direct influence on the division of labour, one could be very optimistic about a more equal division of labour in the Netherlands in the near future. Attitudes towards gender roles and the division of labour in the Netherlands have shifted considerably over the last decades and can now be called progressive. Where the division of labour in families is concerned, the Dutch profess to be very egalitarian: over 70% of them feel that men and women should share domestic tasks equitably, 85% feel that housework is a man's responsibility as much as a woman's, and almost 90% agrees that child care is a man's responsibility as well (SCP, 1994b).

Although ideology in the Netherlands appears to favour those with an egalitarian division of labour, very few people actually experience such a division. The distribution of housework and child care in the Netherlands, as described in the previous section, can be summarized briefly: men spend about half as much time on both housework and child care as women do (De Jong & De Olde, 1994). Consequently, one would expect many couples to experience a discrepancy between theory - their attitudes - and practice. In the remainder of this chapter, we will attempt to shed some light on the ways people deal with (or choose not to deal with) this discrepancy. In order to do that, we will first briefly review the literature on the relationship between gender role attitudes and the division of household labour.

Results from various studies that focus on this relationship indicate that it is not as simple as might be predicted by role theory. Some of the studies relating gender role attitudes to the division of household tasks yielded a positive relationship between more egalitarian attitudes of both partners and a more egalitarian division of household tasks (Stafford,

Backman & Dibona, 1977; Atkinson & Huston, 1984). In a longitudinal study in New Zealand, the gender role attitudes of couples measured shortly before they got married were the best predictor of their actual division of household tasks one year later (Koopman-Boyden & Abbot, 1985). Individuals who indicated a high degree of acceptance of feminist ideology before marriage showed a strong tendency to report less traditional division of household tasks one year after their marriage.

In some other studies, it was found that the attitudes of only one of the partners were related to the division of housework. In two American studies, men with more egalitarian attitudes did more housework than men with traditional attitudes (Antill & Cotton, 1988; Ross, 1987). In these studies the attitudes of the women did not significantly affect the division of tasks. In contrast to these findings, a study by Barnett and Baruch (1987) on determinants of the participation of fathers in household and child care tasks showed that the amount of housework done by the man in dual earner families mainly depended on the gender role attitudes of the wife. In families where the wife did not have a paid job, gender role attitudes of neither husband nor wife were related to the amount of housework performed by the husband. (In these cases, the men's attitudes toward the quality of fathering they had received as children was the best predictor of their participation.) In one study, even a reverse relationship between egalitarian attitudes and sharing of household tasks was reported (Coverman, 1985). There it was found that non-traditional attitudes in men corresponded with less participation in housework.

Apart from a general influence on the sharing of household tasks between partners, gender role attitudes might also influence which tasks are done by whom. Antill and Cotton (1988) made a distinction between household tasks that are perceived to be typically feminine (cleaning, washing) or typically masculine (repairs, car maintenance). Women with more egalitarian attitudes did more of the masculine tasks and less of the feminine tasks than did women with more traditional attitudes, even though their attitudes did not affect the total amount of time they or their husbands devoted to housework.

There are also a few studies that did not relate attitudes to the actual division of housework, but explored the relationships of gender role attitudes with the desired division of tasks, or with the evaluation of the division. In a study done in the Netherlands, De Jong and De Olde (1994) correlated gender role attitudes with the desired division of work of 227 couples with young children. Apart from general gender role attitudes, they also asked for attitudes on more specified topics, such as child care and work. They found that gender role attitudes related more strongly to the desired division of paid labour than to the division of housework. Women's attitudes correlated more strongly to the desired division of work, both paid and unpaid, than those of men. The correlations found by De Jong & De Olde were substantial, but unfortunately they did not relate the attitudes to the actual division of work. Results from a study by Piña and Bengtson (1993) of 283 married women, indicate that full-time working wives with non-traditional attitudes experienced less support from their partner and were less happy when the division of tasks was more unequal, while this relationship did not emerge for either women with traditional attitudes or women who did not have a full-time job. A wife's traditionalism exhibited a stronger legitimating effect in preserving the unequal status quo in households than a wife's non-participation in the (full-time) paid labour force. This indicates that, even though attitudes might not always be related to the actual outcome, they are related to the evaluation of the division and to well-being.

These results show an effect in the predicted direction between attitudes and behaviour, differing only in magnitude. A negative relationship was reported in only one study. However, it is problematic that in some studies only egalitarian gender role attitudes of the wife appeared as a predictor of an egalitarian division of work, while in others, the attitudes of the husband did. A further problem in interpreting these findings is that the studies are difficult to compare, because the samples and the ways in which the gender role attitudes were measured are very divergent. In some cases, the gender role attitudes were based on only a few questions, whereas in other studies lengthy questionnaires were used. Still, there did not seem to be any systematic relationship between differences in measurement and differences in results between the studies. Apart from these measurement issues, it seems that the relationship between gender role attitudes and sharing of housework might be different for different types of families, depending on, for example, whether or not the wife has a job. All in all, the relationship between gender role attitudes and the division of tasks does not seem as straightforward as is sometimes assumed. Moreover, the general pattern in all studies is that the wife does more housework than the husband. So, although in some cases attitudes and behaviour seem to correspond, a gap between agreement with egalitarian gender roles and an unequal division of tasks is evident to a certain extent in most studies.

The attitude-behaviour (in)consistency

The observed gap between attitudes and behaviour is not restricted to the domain of housework. In other areas as well low correlations (or no correlations at all) are found between attitudes and supposedly related behaviour. This is of considerable concern to attitude researchers, for they have traditionally assumed that people use these attitudes to guide their actions. In the 1970s, attitude research was primarily concerned with the question whether or not there *is* a relationship between attitudes and behaviour. To summarize the studies that have tried to answer this question, attitude-behaviour relations can range from no relation at all to very strong correlations. The answer to the question therefore has to be (and this holds true for housework as well, which can be gathered from the discussion of research results in the previous section) 'sometimes.'

The next question that comes to mind is why there is a relation in some cases, but not in others, which is basically the question we are trying to answer here. What factors explain the gap between attitudes and behaviour? Zanna and Fazio (1982) have labelled this the 'when' question: 'under *what conditions* do *what kinds of attitudes* held by *what kinds of individuals* predict *what kinds of behaviour*?' This would indicate four types of factors that may influence the attitude-behaviour relationship, and consequently four types of possible explanations of the inconsistency between attitudes and behaviour. We would like to add a fifth type, suggested by Fazio (1986) that deals with *the way in which attitudes are held*. Fazio calls this the 'how' question: how do attitudes guide behaviour? A final, sixth type concentrates on measurement issues. First we will discuss each of these six types of explanations and consider if and how they might play a role in the discrepancy between theory and practice in the division of labour. Where possible, we have drawn on existing research to support our expectations.

Conditions
The first type of explanation is based on situational factors that influence the attitude-behaviour relation. Several factors have been found to have such an influence. The one we think is particularly relevant in this case is the idea that attitude is pertinent to the behaviourial decision (Snyder & Kendzierski, 1982). An illustration of this might be the phenomenon that general ideas of individuals do not necessarily correspond to what they think is proper for themselves. It is possible that people have norms for their own behaviour that are different from their general views on gender roles. It appears logical that what people think about themselves and the way tasks are divided in their household will be influenced by their adherence to certain gender role attitudes. General opinions may change faster than individual's norms and ideas themselves, however. Moreover, even if general opinions influence on the way people view themselves, they might not be seen as having anything to do with (norms and ideas about) an individual's behaviour.

Types of attitudes
The second type of explanation refers to the specific qualities of certain attitudes. It appears that some are more likely than others to show an attitude-behaviour consistency. Some of these qualities have been identified (for a more complete overview, see Fazio, 1990), for example, the consistency between affective and cognitive components of attitudes. In the case of the division of labour in families, the cognitive and affective components of the attitudes may be incompatible for some. It is conceivable that someone may support egalitarianism on the grounds of fairness, or agree with existing policies (the cognitive component), but that does not mean that this person necessarily *likes* the idea of gender equality. Support for this view was reported in a study by Hochschild (1989), in which she

interviewed and observed several dual earner couples. In some families the wife's paid job was seen as a threat to the husband's identity as a breadwinner, especially when she earned more than he did. The couples compensated for this in the division of tasks at home. He had to do less work because he was nice enough to allow her to work. Although this might be expected for couples with traditional gender role attitudes, Hochschild found indications in her interviews of other cases with a discrepancy between what she called 'shallow ideologies' and 'deep feelings.' These deep feelings, generally formed by early experiences and upbringing, reflected much more conservative values and interfered with the egalitarian attitudes that were rationally adhered to, and often proved more influential with regard to decisions about the division of work. Another quality which we feel might play a role concerns the temporal stability of the attitude. The more stable the attitude the higher the correlation with behaviour. Gender role attitudes are often assumed to be quite stable. But as noted earlier, they have, in fact, changed considerably, perhaps indicating that they are more volatile than is generally assumed.

Types of individuals
There are several personality characteristics that have been found to influence the attitude-behaviour relationship, such as self-monitoring, self-consciousness, and level of moral reasoning (e.g., Snyder, 1982). In the case of explaining discrepancies between gender role attitudes and the division of labour, however, this factor does not seem very useful. There is no reason whatsoever to assume that dual earners with children have different personality characteristics than the rest of the population, and therefore this particular attitude-behaviour discrepancy is unlikely to stem from any specific personality characteristic.

Types of behaviour
The fourth type of explanation that we distinguish concentrates on behavioural characteristics. In order to translate attitudes into behaviour, one has to have the idea that it is possible to act a certain way and that the desired outcome is feasible. Behaviours can be easy or difficult to perform. To be able to behave according to their attitudes, individuals need what Ajzen (1985) called 'volitional control' over their actions. In the case of family work, there may be obstacles that make it difficult to have anything but the traditional arrangement. These obstacles can be external (outside the family) or internal (within the family). Even with egalitarian attitudes couples may not be able to achieve equal division of labour in their family: e.g., consider taxes that benefit single earner households, employer policies that make it difficult to combine paid employment and family work, inadequate child care, etc. Kahn and Crosby (1985), in an article on persistent sex discrimination at work (despite revised attitudes towards working women), concluded that it is generally institutional factors that make that unbiased actions have discriminatory effects. Obstacles may also be present

Dilemma or compromise

within the family, for example, the attitudes of a spouse. Individuals may have different attitudes than their partners and therefore have to strike compromises that suit both partners.

How attitudes are held

A fifth possible explanation has to do with the idea of attitude strength. There is, at this point, no formal definition and it has been operationalized in several ways. A well-known indicator of attitude strength is Fazio's concept of 'attitude accessibility' (Fazio, 1986). The idea is that people differ in the ease with which certain attitudes are accessed. Some people are always aware of a certain attitude, while others are less conscious of the same attitude. The attitude-behaviour relationship then, is stronger when an attitude is more accessible, so, perhaps only people for whom their gender role attitudes are 'chronically salient' will act accordingly. There is a substantial amount of evidence for this hypothesis. For instance, in an experimental study, Branscombe and Deaux (1991) found a stronger correlation between gender role attitudes and related behavioural intentions when the attitudes were made salient before the behaviour, than to when they were not. This suggests that although people might have a clear opinion on certain topics, they do not always think about them and consequently do not always use them to guide their actions. Another strength-related dimension is attitude importance (Boninger, Krosnick & Berent, 1995). People differ in how important certain attitudes are to them. An attitude may be considered personally important by one person and not by the next. There is strong evidence that important attitudes are more stable and have more influence on behaviour than unimportant ones (e.g., Krosnick, 1988). There may be individuals who have an egalitarian opinion on gender roles, but who do not consider these opinions important enough to make their decisions consistent with their attitudes. A related argument is that people have more than one set of attitudes towards most subjects, so that gender role beliefs alone do not decide the issue. Therefore attitudes towards children, work etc. are important as well. Perhaps these other attitudes are contradictory with egalitarian attitudes towards gender roles, in which case, the more important attitude or set of attitudes would 'win out,' and have more influence on the behavioural outcome.

Measurement issues

The sixth and final type of explanation is somewhat different from the others, since it is based on methodological arguments. Ajzen and Fishbein (1977) pointed out that predicting behaviour from attitudes is influenced by the level of specificity of both. General patterns of behaviour are best predicted by general attitudes, while a specific behaviour is best predicted by a specific attitude. In particular, it has been argued that attitudes are often measured on a general level while actions occur in specific situations. Could it be that the gender role attitudes that have been used to predict a specific behaviour (such as an individual's participation in family work) have been too general? Are the general gender role attitudes that are often asked for in questionnaires, simply unfit predictors of specific behaviours regarding the division of tasks? It would seem unlikely that this fully explains the lack of correspondence, since many of the items in gender role questionnaires do address issues concerned with the division of labour; it is generally regarded as a central aspect of gender relations. Moreover, both general and specific gender role attitudes have shifted considerably, while neither seems to have had much of an influence on behaviour. Two additional methodological explanations are given by Kahn and Crosby (1985). The first is response bias. Maybe people are only being socially desirable when they express their progressive gender role attitudes. This does not really solve the attitude-behaviour inconsistency, however. There would still be a discrepancy between theory and practice. The final methodological explanation is sample bias. Perhaps the respondents were not representative of the general population; maybe they were not the same people as those who divide their family work unequally. But again, this explanation does not seem likely. Most of the polls and most of the time use studies have large numbers of respondents.

Accounting for the attitude-behaviour inconsistency

The studies discussed above show the complexity of the attitude-behaviour relationship to the issue of housework. It seems likely that one or more of these general explanations should be able to explain the gap between ideas and practice concerning the division of housework. However, there are not many studies that give an indication as to which explanations are most likely to play a role in this setting. Most of the studies described did not try to explain the difference between the reported attitudes and behaviour. As a result the next part will be exploratory in nature. We think it may be useful to examine what the respondents themselves think of these issues, to try and 'validate' the theoretical explanations. The question we hope to answer is; Which of these explanations do people come up with themselves in talking about their division of labour?

   Which explanation someone uses has consequences for the way in which the gap between their ideas and their behaviour is perceived. For example, an explanation that refers to the control one has over one's behaviour would acknowledge that there is an inconsistency between attitudes and behaviour, whereas an explanation that refers to the level of specificity of each would not. The issues that arise are the following: Do individuals acknowledge this gap between their attitudes and their actual behaviour? Do they feel that there is an inconsistency between the two? We expect that most of the respondents will feel this way. And if they do, there are several ways to deal with the inconsistency. They may choose to solve the dilemma by changing either their attitudes or their behaviour. These are the two strategies proposed by another type of consistency theory, cognitive dissonance theory (Festinger, 1957). This theory states that people will always attempt to close the gap and that these two strategies are the only ways to do so. We believe that there is a third option open to those experiencing such a dilemma. They might not choose to actually solve the dilemma, but turn to one of the explanations we discussed earlier. Using one of these explanations would not make attitudes and behaviour more consistent, but would motivate the inconsistency. This strategy would enable them to leave both their gender role attitudes and their division of labour intact without experiencing too much dissonance. The gap would then be closed verbally, or the dilemma solved theoretically. In the next section, we will explore these questions using qualitative data taken from a study in which 25 dual earner couples were interviewed about their division of labour. We will use the explanations described in this section as a guide in organising the responses and explanations of the respondents. In addition, we will look for explanations other than those mentioned and see if there are any systematic differences between men and women.

Procedure
Semi-structured interviews were conducted with 25 dual earner couples. Husbands and wives were interviewed separately to prevent differences between the opinions or perceptions of spouses being overlooked. The average length of the interviews was one hour. Interview topics included the actual division of labour and (the reasons for) its realization, satisfaction with the situation and preferences. At the end of the interview, several gender role attitudes related to the division of work between men and women were assessed. However, most respondents had already made many attitude statements during the course of the interview. The gender role attitudes held by the participants in this study can be summarized as varying from progressive to extremely progressive. The interviews were recorded and later transcribed. All interviews were conducted by the same person (the first author), to make sure that differences between respondents could not be ascribed to the interviewer.

The respondents
The respondents were 25 working women and their spouses (see also Table 6.2). The average age of the women was 38, the average age of the men was 40. The average number of children per couple was two, with an average age of 7.5. The women were employed for 25.4 hours a week on average, the men for 37.3 hours. The women spent 21.5 hours a week on housework and 27.1 hours on child care; 48.6 hours a week were thus spent on unpaid labour by women. The men spent 12 hours a week on housework and 18.2 hours on child care, which adds up to 30.2 hours a week spent on unpaid labour. If paid and unpaid labour are added up, we see that women have a work week of 74 hours while men work 67.5 hours per week. In other words, women have a work week 6.5 hours longer than

that of the men. Compared to the national average, both men and women in this sample spend more time on unpaid labour; women about 1.5 times as much and men twice as much. This difference between the sample and the national average can be ascribed to the fact that these were all dual earner couples, often with young children.

Table 6.2: Some characteristics of the respondents

	Women	Men
Age	38	40
Years Married	11	11
Number of Children	2	2
Age of Children	7.5	7.5
Hours Paid Employment	25.4	37.3
Hours Housework	21.5	12.0
Hours Child care	27.1	18.2
TOTAL WORK WEEK	74.0	67.5

Closing the gap

Although, as has been discussed, the gap between attitudes and behaviour is a common phenomenon, in the case of the division of labour in Dutch families, it seems especially big. In the previous section several possible explanations were identified to account for this discrepancy. In this section we will see which of the explanations are supported by the interviews.

We have already established the gap between gender role attitudes and the division of labour in this sample. Gender role attitudes were egalitarian, while the division of labour was unequal. We will now turn to the explanations given by the respondents. From the interview transcripts, three ways of dealing with attitude-behaviour inconsistency could be distinguished. These will be discussed and illustrated with interview excerpts. Their place in the more theoretical explanations, as outlined in the previous section, will then be assessed.

Control
The most frequently occurring explanation referred to not having had control over the behaviourial outcomes. In every single interview, statements of this type were found. Apparently couples run into quite a few problems in trying to divide tasks according to their attitudes. We will now take a look at these problems, specifically the types of obstacles

encountered within the family. The following two interview fragments are examples of women with such experiences:

'For years I wasn't satisfied with it, but ... well, apparently it's also a growing process [...] and maybe it's just that you get used to it ... that you don't want to divide things anymore, but simply keep them to yourself. And the other does other things, just leave it like that [...] For years I thought that it was unfair that the organisation turns out to be one person's task. But now I feel like, well, apparently it's not possible any other way.'

'I just want him to do half [of the housework]. That is the demand I make. But well, he doesn't comply, so ... well. I'm not dissatisfied, I've accepted it. I'm not dissatisfied, but ... that's why I've gotten a housekeeper. That's the only thing. I don't feel like ... like I did in the past, that I worked till I was sick and he'd do nothing at all. I'm not doing that anymore.'

This story was quite common among the women. Over half the women interviewed told similar stories about how they once may have had other ideals, but it was not possible to live accordingly, because these ideals were not shared by their husbands. They phrase it as 'having accepted it' and often stress that they are not unhappy, but there was simply no alternative. These women would rather perform most of the housework than (continue to) fight with their husbands. For obvious reasons, not many men used this explanation. However, there was one man who also encountered problems when he and his wife were trying to divide tasks equally, but the problem was located with himself:

'I think it would be better, better for J. [daughter], better for me and better for K. [wife] if it were more equal. The next question of course is, how would you do that, and then you realise that it is quite difficult to divide things completely equally. [...] Yes, you can make all sorts of agreements and you can promise each other a whole lot [...] but that doesn't mean that you realise up front what is happening to you and in your family. So, you can't say that you simply divide the tasks and that's it. It doesn't work that way. It just doesn't. You can say, we'll take turns in getting up at night [for the baby], we've tried that, but after a week I was susceptible to every disease around. I just couldn't do it. And then you find practical solutions that may not be equal.'

Surprisingly, the reverse situation occurred as well. There were some instances in which the wife was the one who obstructed an equal division of labour. Women would say that they had trouble leaving some tasks to others for several reasons: they felt they did a better job than their husbands, because their husbands would take too much time completing the task, or simply because they wanted to do it themselves. Men would say that they were forbidden to do some things (usually the laundry), because they had done a poor job in the past. Not many people mentioned external obstacles, such as employers or other institutional factors to an equal division of housework. A possible explanation for not mentioning these things more often might be that they are taken for granted, they go without saying. Simply by being dual earners, these people have already overcome most of these obstacles.

Another phenomenon that occurred in the interviews has to do with the question of whether or not the couple had control over the situation: every single respondent mentioned that the division of labour, or at least a part of that division, was something they had no influence on. In these instances, no specific obstacles were identified. Instead, the focus was on the lack of control and consequently, the lack of responsibility people felt they had for the existing situation. Men did this more often than women, in fact, some of the interviews with men were no more than a sequence of variations on this theme. The question that prompted most of these utterances was how the current division of labour came to exist. Three responses, the first two by men and the third by a woman follow:

'I don't really remember. I think it just ... happened that way.'

'Oh, we never made any clear arrangement about that. It's something that happens with time. [...] Yes, it just automatically developed in a certain way.'

'It wasn't planned this way, no ... things really arranged themselves this way.'

Both men and women (but especially men) apparently do not believe that the division of labour is something they have helped create. So, if the current division of labour was not influenced by them, they were not responsible for its realization. This line of reasoning implies that there is also not room for change. Perhaps they wouldn't even feel compelled to try a different arrangement, since they don't feel responsible for the current. Whether or not their attitudes are egalitarian or the division of labour is in accordance with their attitudes becomes irrelevant. The gap between attitudes and behaviour is recognized and acknowledged, but there is nothing they can do about it. It seems that there are many things that keep people from arranging their division of labour the way they want to. Some of these are within the individuals themselves, whereas other things are perceived to be beyond their control.

Attitude strength

As was described in the previous section, attitudes and behaviour often correlate more strongly when attitudes are stronger, or more important to someone. In the case of division of tasks in the family this would mean that egalitarian gender role attitudes are not necessarily seen as a factor on which the division of housework and child care should be based. For some people, gender role attitudes are simply not on their minds, or not very important to them personally. Consequently they are not related to their behaviour.

In the interviews, this was expressed poignantly by two men who both thought the division of labour in their families was not in accordance with their attitudes, but were not planning any action to change either their attitudes or their behaviour. Rather, they expected the division to become more equal by itself:

> 'I do think the division is lopsided, but ... no, I wouldn't know what we would change. [It should be] More equal, really, so you have the feeling that you both have an equitable number of tasks. But as far as that goes, at the moment we're in a phase of running and never stopping really. And then you think, there'll be another phase, when things will get quieter. [...] Maybe things will change again, but ... I think that that's at the back of my mind too, like, someday we'll change something, but that means that ... somewhere some initiative will have to be taken.'

> 'Um ... if you say, what could be better about the division, then I could just do some more um ... housework, so to speak. [...] I should do more in the mornings. That we both get up at the same time in the morning and stuff, so we can do that [child care] together. Well, I ... now, what'll I say ... yes, I guess I would want that. I think it will...it happens more and more these days, and eventually it will creep in, that I ... [...] It will happen by itself I guess.

The following is another example of an instance where gender role attitudes are not really important to someone, and definitely do not guide his actions:

> 'Well...sometimes my wife does a little too much. Well, see, I could cook sometimes too, or um ... or something, or do the shopping, but I don't. I simply think, my wife will do that. And that works out fine, so ... But sometimes I think, I could do that every once in a while. It's not that I dislike it or anything.'

This type of explanation was used mostly (but not exclusively) by men. Only a few women regarded their gender role attitudes as not important. For example:

> 'I'm not going to make a big deal out of it, no way. I'm not going to say that he should learn to do the ironing, don't be silly, it's not worth it. I don't think so. [...] I may grumble over it sometimes, of course, but then I think ... oh well, it's just not worth it.'

The fact that men used this strategy more often than women is compatible with results reported by Boninger, Krosnick and Berent (1995), who describe the role of self-interest in determining importance of attitudes to individuals. Even though, in theory, the organisation of housework might be considered as relevant to men as to women, the traditional practice that women have responsibility for these issues probably shapes the attitudes.

In this case, the gap between attitudes and behaviour is acknowledged as well. The difference with the previous section is that in that case, people emphasized not being able to do anything about the situation, whereas in this case they stressed not being willing to change the situation. Apparently, it is possible to live with an inconsistency.

The difference between general ideas and ideas about oneself
Another possible explanation for the fact that couples do not divide their tasks and time according to their attitudes may be the difference between general attitudes and norms for oneself. These might not be the same. The general attitude might be taken to mean a kind of principle that does not necessarily apply to one's personal situation. The following quotes illustrate this difference. The first quote is from a woman, the second from a man.

> 'I believe that if you're both working - and that's what this investigation is about, of course - that the man could do a bit more, yes. But because there isn't enough time that simply doesn't happen. But I think he could do a bit more, certainly if there were more time. Because his job is really busy. And takes up a lot of time, a whole lot. I couldn't even estimate it, maybe 60 or 70 hours, so that the little time he's free, he should relax a bit. And he does try to pay some attention to the family in those few hours, but also to have a little bit for himself.'

> '... So in that sense, I'd say it's not completely fair [...] No, it would be fair if you would do a bit more around the house, but that's not possible. Look, it sort of depends on the job. If your job is only slightly mentally taxing, you could very well summon up some energy for all sorts of other things. If your job is more taxing then you need more time to recharge. That means you spend more time reading and puttering a bit and stuff. And that means you really can't do a lot about it. Yes, you can ... where there's a will there's a way, that's easy enough. But basically it's not that you can say "OK, I'll do a bit more around the house".'

It seems that people, although they have egalitarian attitudes as far as society in general or others are concerned, often see themselves and their own particular situation as exceptional. Individuals who focus on this difference are aware of the inconsistency of theory and practice, and frequently offer lengthy explanations why a more equal division of labour was not possible in their specific situation. As far as changing the division of labour is concerned, this type of explanation is somewhere between the two types discussed earlier. Here, the respondents are not saying they *cannot* change it exactly, but they are not saying they *will not* change it either. Of all the explanations used, this type requires more effort to actually (even if only verbally) close the gap between attitudes and behaviour. The use of language is interesting in these fragments: both use the general and unspecified 'you' when they are really talking about themselves. The use of this word creates a distance between their general attitudes and their own situation.

In closing this section, we would like to address the two strategies (proposed by cognitive dissonance theory) for making attitudes and behaviour consistent. None of the respondents mentioned changing their attitudes. This is not very surprising, for even though gender role attitudes may not be as stable as they are often thought to be, it is not very likely that they will change during an interview. The other option, according to cognitive dissonance theory, is changing one's behaviour. We did find some evidence for this strategy: two of the men mentioned plans for changing their behaviour, that is, for increasing their share of family work. Most of the respondents, however, looked for other ways to make the inconsistency between their ideas and their behaviour more acceptable.

Concluding remarks

The interview results give some support to three of the explanations mentioned: behaviour control, attitude strength, and situational factors. We would like to stress the fact that these are layman's explanations, based on 'common sense.' This would account for the absence of explanations based on attitudinal qualities, since this requires more insight into how attitudes are defined. For obvious reasons, explanations based on personality characteristics or measurement issues are missing as well. People are hardly likely to refer to their own specific personalities, especially when justifying why they do not put their beliefs into practice. As for measurement issues, these were in depth interviews, in which no direct measurement took place. This does not mean that these three types of explanations do not play a role in this setting. It merely means that, given the methodological limitations of this study, we could not find any evidence for them.

Most of the evidence points towards the explanation focusing on restrictions which inhibit a division of labour consistent with people's attitudes: control over the outcomes and, to a lesser extent, conflicting interests between spouses. In cases where people want an equal division of labour in their family, they usually run into problems, one of which can be their spouse. Women in particular often feel that their share of labour is a compromise between their ideals and their husbands. Women, more than men, reported of 'having accepted the situation' or 'having gotten used to it.' A closely connected - though not identical - sentiment is the feeling that every single respondent sooner or later mentioned not having (or having had) any influence on the division of labour. The difference between these two situations lies in how couples perceive (or do not perceive) their influence on the division of labour. In the first case, people (mostly women) realize that the arrangement is something that can be controlled and changed, though they themselves have not succeed in doing so, often because they wanted to avoid conflicts with their spouses. In the second case, individuals actually question the possibility of actively changing the situation. When they say that the situation just happened, that there were no negotiations about the division of labour and things just seemed to arrange themselves in a certain way, they are, in fact, saying that they do not have control over the situation. Also, they are referring to forces outside their own family that prevent a different, more equal, division of labour, or at least encourage and facilitate a traditional distribution of chores.

Influencing the division of labour through influencing gender role attitudes will therefore not be an easy task. All of the respondents acknowledged an inconsistency between their gender role attitudes and their household tasks. And, although awareness is a necessary first step, it is not enough to change behaviour. Even when the respondents were aware of the fact that their attitudes and their behaviour were not consistent, they rarely expressed the need to alter the situation. It appears that such an inconsistency does not necessarily make people uncomfortable. The strength of the attitudes, and the difference between general attitudes and specific ideas about oneself may have something to do with this. As we have seen, (egalitarian) gender role attitudes are just not that important to some people, or are simply not relevant. One might say that these individuals, even though they are aware of the fact that their attitudes and their division of tasks are not consistent, choose not to deal with this inconsistency. In addition, it is not hard for them to justify why a more equal distribution of labour, no matter how much they might want it, is not possible in their own family. All of those interviewed stressed their belief that housework and child care should be divided equally between men and women. It seems that people like to hang on to their egalitarian beliefs, even if it is only to comply with societal norms, to be socially desirable, or to win points with the interviewer. At the same time, no one seemed to have a problem with the basic tenet that attitudes and behaviour should logically be consistent. This accounts for the lengthy explanations some interviewees gave to make clear that their own family was a special case and they should not be judged negatively for saying one thing and doing another. In this sense, the explanations offered by the respondents sometimes sound very much like excuses (Van der Vinne, 1995); the gap between attitudes and behaviour is closed only in a verbal sense.

Finally, a few comments should be made on the usefulness of attitudes in research on the division of labour in families. If the goal is to predict this division, attitudes are not very useful. We have seen that a wide variety of attitudes have been used in previous research, with differing results. In this chapter, we hope to have offered some possible reasons for these contradictory findings. We believe that the context of the family and its division of labour is an interesting one in which to study attitudes. An important question for further research would be, for example, how attitude strength changes over time. It seems that many of the women interviewed who used to have strong ideals with regard to the division of labour, have eventually decided that having a family is more important than sharing family work equally.

References

Ajzen, I. (1985). From intentions to actions: a theory of planned behavior. In J. Kuhl & J. Beckmann (Eds.), *Action-control: from cognition to behavior*, pp. 11-39, Heidelberg: Springer.

Ajzen, I. & M. Fishbein (1977). Attitude behavior relations: a theoretical analysis and review of empirical research. *Psychological Bulletin, 84*, 888-918.

Antill, J. K. & S. Cotton (1988). Factors affecting the division of labor in households. *Sex Roles, 18*, 531-553.

Atkinson, J. & T.L. Huston (1984). Sex role orientation and division of labor in early marriage. *Journal of Personality and Social Psychology, 46,* 330-345.

Barnett, R. C. & G.K. Baruch (1987). Determinants of fathers' participation in family work. *Journal of Marriage and the Family, 49,* 29-40.

Boninger, D.A., J.A. Krosnick & M.K. Berent (1995). Origins of attitude importance: self-interest, social identification, and value relevance. *Journal of Personality and Social Psychology, 68,* 61-80.

Branscombe, N. R. & K. Deaux (1991). Feminist attitude accessibility and behavioral intentions. *Psychology of Women Quarterly, 15,* 411-418.

Coverman, S. (1985). Explaining husbands' participation in domestic labor. *The Sociological Quarterly, 26,* 81-97.

Fazio, R.H. (1986). How do attitudes guide behavior? In R.M. Sorrentino & E.T. Higgins (Eds.), *Handbook of motivation and cognition: foundations of social behavior,* pp. 204-243, New York: Guilford Press.

Fazio, R.H. (1990). Multiple processes by which attitudes guide behavior: the MODE model as an intergrative framework. *Advances in Experimental Social Psychology, 23,* 75-109.

Festinger, L. (1957). *A theory of cognitive dissonance.* Stanford: Stanford University Press.

Hochschild, A. (1989). *The second shift: working parents and the revolution at home.* New York: Viking.

Jong, A. de & C. de Olde (1994). *Hoe ouders het werk delen.* Den Haag: Ministerie van Sociale Zaken en Werkgelegenheid/VUGA.

Kahn, W.A. & F. Crosby (1985). Discriminating between attitudes and discriminatory behaviors. Change and stasis. In L. Lanwood, A.H. Stromberg & B.A. Getuk (Eds.), *Women and work. An annual review, vol. 1.* pp. 215-238. Beverly Hills, CA: Sage Publications.

Koopman-Boyden, P. G. & M. Abbott (1985). Expectations for household task allocation and actual task allocation: a New Zealand study. *Journal of Marriage and the Family, 47,* 211-219.

Krosnick, J.A. (1988). The role of attitude importance in social evaluation: a study of policy preferences, presidential candidate evaluations, and voting behaviour. *Journal of Personality and Social Psychology, 55,* 196-210.

Lippe, T. van der (1993). *Arbeidsverdeling tussen mannen en vrouwen.* Amsterdam: Thesis.

Lippe, T. van der & M. Niphuis-Nell (1994). De taakverdeling thuis, 1975-1990. *Tijdschrift voor Arbeidsvraagstukken, 10,* 266-279.

Piña, D. L. & V.L. Bengtson (1993). The division of household labor and wives' happiness: ideology, employment and perceptions of support. *Journal of Marriage and the Family, 55,* 901-912.

Ross, C. E. (1987). The division of labour at home. *Social Forces, 65,* 816-833.

Smit, J. (1967). Het onbehagen bij de vrouw. *De Gids, 130,* 267-281.

Snyder, M. (1982). When believing means doing: creating links between attitudes and behavior, In M.P. Zanna, E.T. Higgins & C.P. Herman (Eds.), *Consistency in social behavior: the Ontario Symposium* (Volume 2, pp. 105-130), Hillsdale: Erlbaum.

Snyder, M. & D. Kendzierski (1982). Acting on one's attitude: procedures for linking attitude and behavior. *Journal of Experimental Social Psychology, 18,* 165-183.

Stafford, R., E. Backman & P. Dibona (1977). The division of labor among cohabiting and married couples. *Journal of Marriage and the Family, 39,* 42-57.

Sociaal en Cultureel Planbureau (SCP) (1994a). *Sociale Verkenningen 1994.* Rijswijk/Den Haag: Sociaal en Cultureel Planbureau/VUGA.

Sociaal en Cultureel Planbureau (SCP) (1994b). *Sociaal en Cultureel Rapport 1994.* Rijswijk/Den Haag: Sociaal en Cultureel Planbureau/VUGA.

Tweede Kamer (1992/1993). *Beleidsprogramma emancipatie 'Met het oog op 1995.'* Tweede Kamer vergaderjaar 1992/1993, 22913, nrs 1-2. Den Haag: SDU.

Vinne, H. van der (1995). *It is fair because we both agree that housework is her job: on the division of housework and child care among dual earners in the Netherlands.* Paper presented at the Fifth International conference on Social Justice Research, Reno, June 26-29.

Zanna, M.P. & R.H. Fazio (1982). The attitude-behavior relation: moving toward a third generation of research. In M.P. Zanna E.T. Higgins & C.P. Herman (Eds.), *Consistency in social behavior: the Ontario Symposium* (Volume 2, pp. 283-301). Hillsdale: Erlbaum.

7

Equal opportunities policy:
A solution to the dilemmas in young women's lives

Saskia Keuzenkamp

Introduction

The previous chapters have shown that combining paid and unpaid labour is still far from plain sailing for women in the Netherlands despite the fact that the Dutch government has been pursuing an equal opportunities policy for no less than two decades. This policy is aimed at broadening women's options. The government strives to offer everyone, irrespective of gender or marital status, the opportunity to earn their own living and to exercise equal rights, opportunities, individual choice and equal responsibilities. Allowing women to achieve greater economic independence by taking part in paid employment is a crucial aspect of this equal opportunities policy. The Dutch government also pursues a population policy. Although the policy is not explicitly pronatalist, the government does stress that (heterosexual) couples should not encounter any obstacles if they wish to have children. It sees policy in support of women's emancipation, namely measures that create the necessary conditions for women to combine paid labour with child care, as an important instrument to this end. Still, it is far from clear what the actual effect of equal opportunities policy is. To what extent are women's options broadened, and what will women's lives look like in the future if an effective equal opportunities policy is pursued? I shall try to shed light on this issue in this chapter by providing an answer to the following question: What will be the long-term effects of a number of different equal opportunities policy measures aimed at extending the economic independence of women on their labour force participation and family formation? I shall focus on young women born between 1964 and 1969 since they still have to make a choice between paid and unpaid labour, or a combination thereof.

In this chapter I shall first give an overview of current knowledge regarding the impact of different policy measures on female labour force participation and family formation and discuss the shortcomings of existing research literature on these issues. I shall then explain the manner in which I studied and assessed the effects of government policy in support of women's emancipation. I made a distinction between three types of women, based on their 'family and job aspirations': job-oriented, combination-oriented and motherhood-oriented. A panel of experts were asked (in a so-called Delphi project) to assess the effects of different policy scenarios on the course of life of the three types of women mentioned. The policy scenarios studied were: extending child care facilities and maternity and parental leave schemes; a more flexible organisation of paid labour; and the individualisation of incomes. I shall then present the results of the expert consultation and draw a number of conclusions.

Effects of policy measures: existing literature

Existing literature on the impact of policy measures which are being implemented or advocated in support of women's emancipation focuses on various types of measures: an extension of child care facilities, improvement of maternity and parental leave schemes, a more flexible organisation of paid labour and the individualisation of incomes. All these measures are aimed at removing any obstacles which women might encounter when entering the labour market or pursuing a career by enabling them to combine paid and unpaid labour. These policy measures also affect men since they allow them to spend more time on unpaid labour. Measures regarding the individualisation of incomes are slightly different from the three other types of policy measures since they do not deal with 'organisational' matters but with women's financial circumstances.

A study of literature shows that an extension of *child care facilities* will stimulate the labour force participation of women. This conclusion has been drawn on the basis of surveys carried out among women. The women studied indicated that they would (continue to) work, and work more hours a week, if adequate child care were available (Wilbrink-Griffioen, 1987; Ministerie van WVC, 1992). Similar conclusions can be drawn from comparative studies in different countries (Bruyn-Hundt & Van der Linden, 1989; Eggink, Van Praag & Hop, 1990). This would give women who have children or who are considering having children the option to remain active in the labour market.

The effects of an extension of child care facilities on family formation are not as clear. Some authors believe that better child care would remove a major obstacle to parenthood: it makes it easier to combine a job with having children. This could have a pronatalist effect (Van der Hoeven, Leeuw & Mesman-Schulz, 1988; Frinking, 1990). Research carried out in Sweden seems to support this conclusion, although the researcher draws attention to the fact that this does not mean that the conclusion always applies in other countries. 'For example, in countries where it is considered as being preferable for a woman to withdraw from the labour market to look after pre-school children, an extensive child-care leave might be more effective' (Gauthier, 1992; p. 10). Heitlinger points out that certain measures may have both a pronatalist and an antinatalist effect, the net result being zero. 'To the extent that child care availability increases women's entry into paid employment, it may be antinatalist, but to the extent that it reduces the burden of child rearing for those who are, and will remain, in the labour force, it may be pronatalist' (Heitlinger, 1991, p. 370).

A study of literature shows that an extension of *different types of leave* will presumably have no more than a minor impact on women's lives. The quality and availability of maternity and parental leave schemes appear to be of little influence on decisions regarding labour force participation and family formation. Research shows that factors such as the quality of one's working environment and the appeal of one's job have a greater impact on labour force participation than the availability of leave schemes as such (Van Amstel, 1992). Moreover, whereas leave schemes may offer temporary relief, they do not provide a structural solution to combining a paid job with children. Women tend to remain in the labour force if they are offered paid maternity leave; they tend to quit their jobs if this is not the case (Pelzer & Miedema, 1990; Ministerie SZW, 1994). As for the impact of leave schemes on family formation, research shows that there is no reason to believe that the average number of children per family will be affected. It is possible, however, that the timing of births will change; that is to say, that couples will have children at an earlier age (Bosman, 1989; Gauthier, 1992). Elchardus and Martin (1985) question whether this will be the case. They doubt whether women with good jobs will actually take the leave they are entitled to.

The concept of *a more flexible organisation of paid labour* is used to denote a wide range of facilities, including: flexitime, cuts in working hours and giving people more say in when they want to work, voluntary and reversible part-time work, various types of leave, and prolonged career interruptions for the purpose of raising children. Little is known about the effects of greater flexibility on women's lives, but we do know that there is a demand for variable and/or shorter working hours per day among parents with young children (Rozendal, Moors & Leeuw, 1985; Pelzer & Miedema, 1990). This finding is confirmed by Van Amstel (1992) who states that greater flexibility plays an important role in women's decisions whether or not to continue working after the birth of a child. It is not clear whether greater flexibility also has an impact on women's decisions regarding family formation. Sundström and Stafford (1992) and Gauthier (1992) tackle this question using data from Sweden. Sundström and Stafford (1992) state that flexitime combined with ample facilities for maternity and parental leave and subsidised daycare have lowered the cost of having children. They draw the conclusion that Sweden's relatively large average family size may be attributed in part to the availability of these facilities. Gauthier (1992), on the other hand, argues that greater flexibility and an extension of leave schemes merely affect the timing of births since women are less inclined to delay childbirth.

Existing literature on the impact of *the individualisation of incomes* indicates that such policy measures boost female labour force participation (Bruyn-Hundt & Van der Linden, 1989; Sundström & Stafford 1992). Financial incentives based on this policy would make it financially more attractive for women to participate in the labour market.

I have not come across any literature on the effects of such a policy scenario on family formation. There is, however, ample literature on the impact of measures aimed at lowering the cost of having children, such as benefits at childbirth, tax incentives for parents with children, child allowance, etc. Several authors argue that these types of measures result in a higher average number of children per woman (Ekert, 1986; Blau & Robins, 1989; Gauthier, 1992). But the effect is minimal. Gauthier, for example, states that 'increasing direct cash transfers by 25% (from their average value) would increase total fertility rate by 0.02 child per woman' (Gauthier, 1992, p. 20). Her calculation is based on research conducted in 22 countries. Other publications indicate that such measures affect the timing of births in addition to the average family size. Ermisch (1991), for example, points out that in the United Kingdom higher financial benefits and premiums influence family size since they encourage women to conceive a third or fourth child and to have children at an earlier age.

These insights into the impact of cash benefits on family formation can be used to assess the effects of the individualisation of incomes. We may then assume that such individualisation would increase the financial benefits of having a job. Women who do not participate in the labour market suffer a loss of income. This raises the cost of having children, which could mean that women choose to have fewer children (fewer third and fourth children) and that they will be inclined to delay motherhood.

On the basis of existing literature we may draw the conclusion that all these policy measures influence women's lives, in particular their labour force participation. As far as we know, the impact on family formation - the number of children, the timing of births, or both - is rather small.

This conclusion has to be qualified, however. First of all, the effects of given measures are assessed more or less in isolation: researchers analyse either the impact on labour force participation or the impact on family formation. We may assume, however, that the choices women make during the course of their lives are interrelated. It would therefore be more useful to study these issues in conjunction with one another. Secondly, many studies compare countries where these measures form part of a total package of government policy measures (quite apart from the fact that each country has a culture of its own). It is difficult to determine the exact effects of a single policy measure. A third observation which has to be made is that most studies ignore the fact that women do not constitute a homogeneous group (see also: Gauthier, 1993). Even within one and the same country, women from different 'categories' have different rights to certain facilities (such as tax relief, maternity leave and child care). Moreover, the extent to which women actually make use of the available facilities also differs. On top of that, women do not have equal access to additional facilities, such as special benefits offered by employers. Lastly, even if all women (or households) had equal access to benefits and facilities and would make equal use of them in absolute terms, their relative value would still not be the same for every individual. For example, the importance of financial incentives depends on the total household budget. In view of the above, the conclusions presented in the available literature on the subject need to be interpreted with due caution.

A scenario project

We drew up a scenario project in order to assess the effects of equal opportunities policy on the lives of women (born between 1964 and 1969). The project consists of four steps: making a fundamental analysis, drawing up policy scenarios, developing a context scenario, and analysing the effects of various policy scenarios (for a detailed description, see Keuzenkamp, 1995).

During the fundamental analysis we developed a typology of women with the aid of a study of literature and a secondary analysis of data taken from the 1988 Fertility Survey conducted by the Netherlands Central Bureau of Statistics (Centraal Bureau voor de Statistiek, 1990). This enabled us to analyse the effects of different policy scenarios on different types of women. The women were classified on the basis of the (latent) variable 'family and job aspirations,' yielding three types of women: job-oriented, combination-oriented and motherhood-oriented women. Job-oriented women (16% of all women studied) have a relatively high level of education and are more interested in paid employment than the two other categories of women. They are generally in favour of combining motherhood and work, although two-fifths of these women believe they will remain childless. Combination-oriented women (49% of all women) have generally completed secondary education. They are also in favour of working mothers, but in their personal lives they say the decision whether they will return to work after childbirth depends on the situation at home. All combination-oriented women plan to have children. Motherhood-oriented women (36% of all women) say women should stay at home to raise their children and they put the family first in their own lives. These women have a relatively low level of education. The family and job aspirations of the different types of women just described coincide with a specific course of life. This will be discussed in more detail later on. When analysing the effects of equal opportunities policy one should note that such a policy can have both a direct and an indirect impact on the behaviour of women. The indirect consequences are the result of the fact that the family and job aspirations of women are affected; these aspirations, in their turn have an effect on the typology of women (for example, an increase in the percentage of job-oriented women). Direct consequences arise when the behaviour of the different types of women changes, for example when a growing percentage of combination-oriented women return to work after the birth of their first child.

We then drew up three policy scenarios (child care and maternity/parental leave, greater flexibility, and the individualisation of incomes) and a context scenario. The child care and leave-of-absence policy is aimed at enabling women to combine paid employment with child care by improving the range of facilities such as daycare and paid maternity leave, and the introduction of so-called emergency leave. Government policy aimed at achieving greater flexibility is based on the idea that every working person also has domestic responsibilities.

This scenario includes policy measures such as cuts in working hours (a 32-hour working week), the introduction of a legal right to part-time work, and giving individuals more say in when they wish to work. Under the individualisation scenario, income regulations are changed such that the level of an individual's income is based on his specific situation only. The possible presence of a partner is not taken into account. This scenario includes measures such as the abolition of transferable tax relief, the abolition of the Additional Benefits Act and various 'free' insurances, and the introduction of an individual right to state benefits. The effects of these policy scenarios were studied on the assumption that major trends in society remain constant. For this purpose, we drew up a context scenario outlining expected socio-economic trends (employment growth, a drop in unemployment, a decrease in the burden of public expenses), and socio-cultural trends (such as continued individualisation, a more pluralist society and a more positive attitude towards women's emancipation).

A Delphi project was set up in order to gain insight into the effects of equal opportunities policy on women's lives. The Delphi method is used to allow a select panel of anonymous experts to arrive at a common judgement without direct contact between them. The participating experts are asked to fill out several questionnaires in a number of consecutive rounds. In each new round, they are presented with the views of the other experts who were consulted in previous rounds. The anonymity of the experts is vital since the participants are not influenced by the possible authority of certain panel members and they are less likely to display modesty simply because they hold certain other panel members in awe. Anonymity also makes it easier for participants to stick to their own points of view and to adjust or qualify their viewpoints, if desired. After all, they can not lose face. On top of that, power struggles and conflicts of interest play a less prominent role than would be the case in face-to-face meetings. Needless to say, the selection of panel members influences the outcome of the project. It is crucial that they are selected in such a way that the panel as a whole has sufficient insight into the different issues dealt with in the project. All aspects of the issues under investigation must be covered, and both general and specialist knowledge of the various aspects must be guaranteed. According to Van Houten (1985) the panel should include users from the general public as well as scholars. After all, consumers are able to assess the consequences of certain policy measures on the basis of personal experience. A total of 36 experts took part in the project, ranging from scholars (universities and research institutes) to 'experiential experts' (trade unions, family council, women's groups, etc.)

The experts in the Delphi project were presented with three policy scenarios, a context scenario and a typology of women. For the sake of comparison, the panel were given an outline of the life histories up to the time of the interview (1988) of the same three categories of women from an older birth cohort (born between 1950 and 1956). The course of these women's lives can be summarised as follows. Job-oriented women are generally active in the labour market or else they are preparing themselves for a paid job. A large majority of these women have no children. Divorce and extramarital cohabitation are more common among these women than among women in the two other categories. Combination-oriented women are generally married and have children. Half these women have a paid job, more often than not part-time. One third of the women in this category are full-time housewives. Motherhood-oriented women, too, are usually married and have children. An overwhelming majority are full-time housewives, one quarter have a job. Important transitions in the lives of these three types of women take place at different points in time. Motherhood-oriented women experience major transitions early in life. Job-oriented women make important transitions later in life. They complete their education later, they marry later, they get their first child later, etc.

Experts on the impact of policy

In order to gain insight into the impact of policy on the lives of all women born between 1964 and 1969, I shall first summarise what the effects are on the distribution of women across the three categories mentioned and on the lives of women within the individual categories. I shall then outline the combined effects of government policy on the average course of life of all women born between 1964 and 1969. Table 7.1 gives an overview of the expected effects of the various policy scenarios. The three categories of women are dealt with separately. No distinction was made between the categories if the panel of experts felt there was no significant difference between them.

Change of mentality
The experts are of the opinion that all three policy scenarios will have an impact on the family and job aspirations of women. Although the policy measures primarily affect the organisation of paid employment and child care within society as a whole, they also influence women's individual attitudes. In other words, government policy is likely to trigger a change of mentality. One of the most striking findings of the panel's investigations is that the attitudes of motherhood-oriented women are most strongly affected and they are becoming more inclined to enter the labour market. This trend may largely be attributed to the growing acceptance of working mothers.

This change of mentality will result in a shift in the size of the three categories of women. The size of the category of job-oriented women will remain unchanged, but the category of combination-oriented women is expected to grow at the expense of the group of motherhood-oriented women. We can not say with certainty what the size of the different categories will be since the respondents were given considerable leeway in the answers provided in the questionnaire (a variation of between 5 and 15 percentage points). However, the experts drew attention to the fact that women are unlikely to change their attitudes following the introduction of the policy scenarios and that a 5-percent shift within a single birth cohort is quite considerable. We may thus conclude that any shifts that take place will be small. This gives the following distribution: 16% of the women are job-oriented (no change), 54% are combination-oriented (plus 5%), and 31% are motherhood-oriented (minus 5%).

Changes in the lives of job-oriented, combination-oriented and motherhood-oriented women
The lives of *job-oriented women* remain relatively unaffected by the different policy scenarios. The only thing which changes in this category are a number of aspects of family formation as a result of child care and leave schemes and possibly also as a result of government policy aimed at greater flexibility. Job-oriented women tend to have their first child between six and eighteen months earlier when such policies are implemented. This trend towards earlier parenthood leads to a slight decline in childlessness. After all, since women have children at an earlier age, involuntary childlessness is less common. According to the panel, the ratio between the number of small families (1 or 2 children) and big families (3 or more children) is not likely to change. The labour force participation of job-oriented women remains practically unchanged. The experts say this may be attributed to the fact that many job-oriented women already have a paid job in the current situation, irrespective of whether they have children. Those women who find it a problem to combine work with children tend to solve this problem by having children at a more advanced age, or not at all. Thanks to government policy aimed at providing child care facilities, leave schemes and possibly even greater flexibility, such solutions are no longer the only way out.

For the category of *combination-oriented women* we can conclude that their lives will be affected considerably by the different policy scenarios. These are the women who want to combine a job with children and who would benefit from policy measures which would broaden their options. According to the panel, the labour force participation of this group of women increases in all three scenarios since a growing number of combination-oriented women (more than half) do not give up their job following the birth of their first child. This increase is clearest when child care facilities and leave schemes are improved. The time these women spend on their jobs also increases: most women have a substantial part-time job (between 20 and 32 hours). Another effect of the introduction of child care facilities, leave schemes and greater flexibility in the organisation of paid employment among combination-oriented women is that they tend to have their first child six to eighteen months earlier, as is the case in the group of job-oriented women. And for this group too, the strategy of delaying childbirth as a (temporary) solution to their dilemma is no longer necessary. The three policy scenarios do not influence other aspects of family formation among combination-oriented women. The degree of childlessness remains the same -

contrary to the group of job-oriented women, these women were never inclined not to have children - as does the ratio between the number of small and big families.

The three policy scenarios also affect the labour force participation of *motherhood-oriented women*, albeit less strongly than among the group of combination-oriented women. A greater number of women remain active in the labour market following the birth of their first child. The percentage is still low, though: less than half. The main reason why the labour force participation of these women increases, is that there is a growing acceptance of working mothers in the new situation. Still, many women give up their jobs following the birth of their first child because of the (lack of) quality of their jobs and low pay, the contacts they have at home, and the satisfaction which children bring. The individualisation policy results in the greatest growth in female labour force participation. It is generally not a matter of choice, however, but is done out of financial necessity. Among motherhood-oriented women, the increased labour force participation which results from certain policy measures does not lead to changes in family formation. Motherhood-oriented women are intent on having children. The government policies outlined in the foregoing have no effect on this desire.

The combined effects on the average course of young women's lives
What are the combined effects of government policy on the average course of life of all three categories of women born between 1964 and 1969? On the one hand we see that certain effects on their lives cancel each other out as a result of shifts within the typology of women, whilst on the other hand certain effects are bigger than they appear at first glance. As we shall see later on, shifts between the three categories of women caused by the implementation of certain policies results in greater changes than the table suggests at first glance. The reader is reminded, however, that these shifts are relatively small: a 5-percent increase in the number of combination-oriented women compared with the number of motherhood-oriented women.

The *labour force participation* of women born between 1964 and 1969 is expected to rise. The Delphi project has shown that the participation rate of combination-oriented and motherhood-oriented women will grow by between 5 and 15 percentage points as a result of the implementation of the various policy scenarios. This growth may be attributed primarily to the fact that more women continue to work following the birth of the first child.

Since combination-oriented women are more inclined to do so than motherhood-oriented women in any case (as shown by the situation of the older birth cohort), the shift of part of the motherhood-oriented women to the group of combination-oriented women means that the increased female labour force participation is even bigger.

In order to assess the overall effect of government policy on *family formation*, I shall deal with the timing of the birth of the first child, childlessness and the ratio between small and

Table 7.1: An overview of the impact of various policy scenarios

	Child care/Leave	Flexibility	Individualisation
Size of category:			
- Job-oriented	≈	≈	≈
- Combination-oriented	↑	↑	↑
- Motherhood-oriented	↓	↓	↓
Labour force participation:			
- Job-oriented	≈	≈	≈
- Combination-oriented	↑ (↑↑)	↑	↑
- Motherhood-oriented	↑	↑	↑
Paid work after first child:			
- Job-oriented	≈	≈	≈
- Combination-oriented	↑	↑	↑
- Motherhood-oriented	↑	↑	↑
Time spent on job:			
- Job-oriented	≈	≈	≈
- Combination-oriented	↑	↑	↑
- Motherhood-oriented	≈	≈	≈
Timing first child:			
- Job-oriented	↓	(↓)	≈
- Combination-oriented	↓	↓	≈
- Motherhood-oriented	≈	≈	≈
Childlessness:			
- Job-oriented	(↓)	(↓)	≈
- Combination-oriented	≈	≈	≈
- Motherhood-oriented	≈	≈	≈
Small families:	≈	≈	≈
Big families:	≈	≈	≈

Key

↑ = expected growth between 5 and 15 percentage points, or postponement by 6 months or more

↓ = expected decline between 5 and 15 percentage points, or brought forward by 6 months or more

≈ = no, or very little change expected

(↑) = an equal number of experts expect no change if ↑

(↓) = an equal number of experts expect no change if ↓

(↑↑) = almost half the experts expect growth by more than 15 percentage points big families.

Among the category of job-oriented women, which is expected to grow following the implementation of the three policy scenarios, the *birth of the first child* will take place earlier as a result of policy measures aimed at providing child care facilities and leave schemes and possibly also as a result of greater flexibility in the organisation of paid labour. Since the size of the group of job-oriented women is not expected to change, there are no cumulative effects. The timing of the birth of the first child will also change among combination-oriented women as a result of both child care and leave schemes and greater flexibility. Since the group of combination-oriented women will grow at the expense of motherhood-oriented women, the effects are cumulative. The fact that the group of combination-oriented women is likely to grow means that the birth of the first child will be postponed. After all, combination-oriented women have their first child about 16 months later in life than motherhood-oriented women. At the same time, however, the result of these policy scenarios is that women decide to have their first child six to eighteen months earlier in life. The end result will, of course, depend on the degree to which women have children at an earlier age. If they have their first child eighteen months earlier, combination-oriented and motherhood-oriented women will have their first child at approximately the same age, and the shifts between the categories will have no effect whatsoever on family formation. However, if the first child is born six months earlier in life, changes in the size of the categories of women do have an impact on family formation. The average age at which women have children rises as a result of the fact that the size of the group of combination-oriented women grows. This effect is somewhat tempered, however, since conception among women in this category generally takes place six months earlier in their lives.

If we take the medium variant, namely bringing the timing of birth among combination-oriented women forward by one year, we can draw the following conclusion: child care facilities, leave schemes and greater flexibility result in an increase in the average age at which all women born between 1964 and 1969 have children since a shift takes place within the typology of women, but this effect is slightly cancelled out by the fact that job-oriented women have children at an earlier age.

The individualisation policy does not have a direct impact on the timing of first births within the three categories of women. It does, however, lead to an increase in the average age at which women have children since the category of combination-oriented women shows some growth. The effect of the individualisation scenario is even stronger than that of the two other policy scenarios since it is not 'tempered' by the fact that women have their first child at an earlier age.

The panel of experts believe that earlier parenthood among job-oriented women will go hand in hand with a slight decrease in *childlessness*. Since this effect only occurs among job-oriented women and since this group is relatively small (16% of all women), and remains small following the implementation of the policy scenarios, the change in the total percentage of childless women will be rather insignificant.

Lastly, a few words regarding the expectation that none of the three policy scenarios will have an impact on the numbers of *small and big families* within the categories of women. When this finding is combined with the expected shifts within the typology, we see that the number of big families (3 or more children) is likely to drop slightly. After all, the life histories of the older cohort indicated that motherhood-oriented women tend to have bigger families than combination-oriented women. Since some of the motherhood-oriented women become combination-oriented, the total number of women with a small family will rise.

Conclusion

In summary, we can say that emancipation policies in support of women's greater economic independence have various effects on young women's lives. If we disregard the differences between policy measures and between the three categories of women, the following conclusion can be drawn. If the government policies outlined are pursued, more women will continue to work following the birth of the first child and they will generally work more hours per week. The timing of first births will be delayed. Childlessness will decline somewhat (albeit only very slightly) and the number of big families (3 or more children) will decrease. These effects may largely be attributed to the fact that all three policy scenarios broaden women's options, enabling them to combine paid employment with children. This is of particular importance to combination-oriented women who face the greatest dilemmas in their efforts to realise their family and job aspirations.

It would be interesting to know which policy scenario is most effective in resolving the 'combination dilemma.' It is not possible, however, to answer that question on the basis of the survey conducted since the questionnaire gave the respondents considerable leeway in their answers. Moreover, the three policy scenarios each solve different aspects of the problem. Some experts say greater flexibility is the most effective policy measure since it offers the most structural solution to combining a paid job with child care. Others, however, say that in this scenario much depends on the role of the male partner, if present, and that women are becoming less dependent on his contribution to child care as a result of the implementation of child care and maternity leave schemes. Policy measures geared towards individualisation are least effective. Paid employment is a more attractive option to women since financial obstacles to entering the labour market are removed (the financial motivation changes). This does not, however, solve the combination problem; it may even exacerbate the problem for some women. The increased labour force participation resulting from this policy scenario may largely be attributed to the fact that some women have to continue working following childbirth out of financial necessity. Several experts draw attention to the fact that equal opportunities policy is most effective if all three policy scenarios are implemented simultaneously since they each solve a different aspect of the problem. This conclusion supports the policy of the present Dutch government which has committed itself to developing an 'integrated approach to employment and care, social security and tax legislation.'

References

Amstel, R.J. van (1992). *Evaluatie van de nieuwe regeling voor zwangerschaps- en bevallingsverlof voor vrouwen in loondienst.* Den Haag: VUGA.

Blau, D.M. & P.K. Robins (1989).'Fertility, employment and Child-care Costs'. *Demography,Vol. 26,* 2, 287-299.

Bosman, E. (1989). 'De demografische (on)doeltreffendheid van maatregelen gericht op het harmoniseren van ouderschap en buitenshuisarbeid van de vrouw'. *Bevolking en Gezin, 3,* 1-30.

Bruyn-Hundt, M. & D. van der Linden (1989). *De invloed van materiële prikkels op het arbeidsaanbod van vrouwen.* OSA-werkdocument nr. 65. Den Haag: OSA.

Centraal Bureau voor de Statistiek (1990). *Onderzoek gezinsvorming 1988. Samenwonen, trouwen, geboorteregeling, werken en kinderen krijgen.* Den Haag: SDU.

Eggink, E., B.M.S. Praag & J.P. Hop (1990). 'Een nieuwe kijk op de arbeidsmarktparticipatie van vrouwen'. *Economisch Statistische Berichten, 1-8-1990.*

Ekert, O. (1986). 'Effets et limites des aides financières aux familles: un expérience et un modèle'. *Population, vol. 41,* 2, 327-348.

Elchardus, M. & A. Martin (1985). 'De beroepsverbondenheid van vrouwen: de invloed van de takenstructuur, van de mate van gecontroleerdheid en van andere eigenschappen van de arbeidssituatie' *Bevolking en Gezin, 3,* 311-335.

Ermisch, J.F. (1991). *Lone Parenthood; An Economic Analysis.* Cambridge: Cambridge University Press.

Frinking, G.A.B. (1990). 'Kiezen voor kinderen. De rol van de overheid ter discussie.' *Gezin, vol. 2, no. 2.*

Gauthier, A.H. (1992). *Does state support for working parents have an effect on fertility? An econometric analysis of the Swedish case.* (Paper prepared for the 1992 ESPE-conference).

Gauthier, A.H. (1993). Families and welfare benefits: the measured and unmeasured effects. In A. Kuijsten (Ed.), *Family structure and family policy* (PDOD-paper no. 17), pp. 1-28. Amsterdam: PDOD.

Heitlinger, A. (1991). 'Pronatalism and women's equality policies'. *European Journal of Population, 7,* 343-375.

Hoeven, E. van der, F.L. Leeuw & K. Mesman-Schulz (1988). *Buitenschoolse opvang van kinderen. Resultaten van een onderzoek naar de achtergronden van en beleid inzake kinderopvang.* Leiden: DSWO Press.

Houten, H.J. van (1985). 'Beleidsgericht Delphi-onderzoek: voorspelling of anticipatie?' *Tijdschrift voor Agologie, 2,* 106-131.

Keuzenkamp, S. (1995). *Emancipatiebeleid en de levensloop van vrouwen. Een toekomst-analyse.* Amsterdam: Babylon-De Geus.

Ministerie van Sociale Zaken en Werkgelegenheid (1994).'Evaluatieverslag ouderschapsverlof.' In *Voortgangsrapportage inzake de positie van vrouwen in de arbeid.* (Bijlage 3 van het rapport). Den Haag: Ministerie van Sociale Zaken en Werkgelegenheid.

Ministerie van Welzijn, Volksgezondheid en Cultuur (1992). *Stimuleringsbeleid Kinderopvang 1990-1993. Resultaten over 1990 en 1991.* Rijswijk: Ministerie van Welzijn, Volksgezondheid en Cultuur.

Pelzer, A. & N. Miedema (1990). *Kinderopvang in Nederland, de FNV-enquête.* Amsterdam: Stichting FNV-pers / Jan Mets.

Rozendal, P.J., H.G. Moors & F.L. Leeuw (1985). *Het bevolkingsvraagstuk in de jaren '80: opvattingen over overheidsbeleid.* Voorburg: NIDI.

Sundström, M. & F. Stafford (1992). 'Female labour force participation, fertility and public policy in Sweden.' *European Journal of Population, 8,* 199-215.

Wilbrink-Griffioen, D., I. van Vliet & A. Elzinga (1987). *Kinderopvang en de arbeidsparticipatie van vrouwen.* Den Haag: Ministerie van Sociale Zaken en Werkgelegenheid.

8

Towards new patterns of division of work in families?

Gerard Frinking
Tineke Willemsen

Introduction

The focus of this book is the study of dilemmas. From a variety of perspectives, we have shown that, in the last decades, changes in family life have presented men and women with difficult choices. These changes are defined in terms of paid and unpaid work. In the various chapters, the different aspects of the choice issue confronting the modern family have been dealt with. Various topics have been addressed: At what point are families first confronted with new dilemmas? How do couples perceive the division of work and care? What solutions are found if the traditional distribution of tasks is not considered viable? What explanation do they give for their task division? Is government policy, specifically equal opportunity policy, able to create the necessary conditions for men and women to make their own choices?

In this chapter an attempt will be made to place the results in a broader perspective. We will try to clarify how the outcome of the decision-making process as it relates to the division of labour in the family, is linked to a specific mode of societal 'regulation.' In line with the theoretical framework developed by the French sociologist Marie-Agnès Barrère-Maurisson, we will argue that some of the dilemmas, which arise in Dutch society, may be due to the social, economic, and institutional forces that characterise the current work and family relations in this society.

Finally, we will devote attention to dilemmas of modern family life in the future. Can we expect that, as a result of the new patterns of division of work, difficult choices, especially for women, will become less prevalent in the next decade, or will families experience the same dilemmas as they do today? What role do policies play in this regard?

Main results of the study

The historical analysis of motherhood and employment careers, in particular the intensity and timing aspects of these two phenomena, has shown how the profile of post-war generations of women has changed over time. Gradually, under the influence of cultural and economic trends, dual careers in families have become more and more manifest. The analysis of motherhood profiles gives some indications that women born after 1945 have postponed (or even given up) motherhood due to the fact that cultural and institutional constraints prevented them from having children at the usual younger ages. This tendency coincides with a periodic 'response' around the year 1975. We can identify the last twenty years as the period in which families had to cope with the new 'combination' problem. A comparison of the different employment profiles, according to the number of working hours in this period, reveals a remarkable stability of working patterns: low incidence of full-time work and high incidence of part-time work.

Heleen van Luijn's study on the ambivalent desire for children, revealed that approximately 15 percent of Dutch women between the ages of 20 and 40 have had doubts about having children for at least one year. For many women in this group, their ambivalence can be traced to the difficulties of combining paid work and child care. Childhood experiences and their partner's attitude towards having children also play a role. The (relative) intensity, duration, and nature of their indecision show that even the large-scale participation in part-time work by women in Dutch society is not a panacea. There are two areas which offer the potential for reducing this ambivalence: expansion of government measures which would make it easier for women to combine work outside the home with child care, plus a change in men's behaviour in raising and caring for children, one that would be more consistent with their progressive attitudes.

In the study on the dilemmas of women with various levels of education, we observe that part-time work is almost without exception preferred by all women across all education levels, when they become mothers. However, there are differences in practice. More highly educated women have more autonomy and (therefore) more opportunities to combine work and family according to their own preferences. For women of intermediate and lower educational levels the opportunities are more restricted. These women more often have to accept working hours which are not always very satisfactory. Few of the more highly educated women succeeded in 'bringing in' the partner as a successful strategy.

Fatherhood has, in recent years, received special attention: the father's role is taken more seriously. An important question is to what degree the 'new' father has entered daily life? Men are no longer exempt from changes in their life pattern, as a result of increased individualism, changed labour relations, and the women's movement. It seems that more and more fathers will experience the same dilemmas as their spouses, especially with the birth of their first child and, for some, after divorce. However, in spite of their progressive attitudes, a large majority of men are reluctant to become too involved in housework and child care. At the same time, we have seen that attitudes are not very useful in explaining the unequal division of work in families. We therefore have to study, in more detail, the division of work in different types of families in order to unravel the impact of, on the one hand, constraints and opportunities of the families and, on the other hand, the aspirations and the strategies of husbands and wives in relation to their practices.

In the context of Dutch society, it is highly improbable that the implementation of new policies with regard to the conciliation between work and family will generate considerable changes in the division of work. But, to some extent, new initiatives, like the introduction of paid parental leave in the market sector, may help to reevaluate family life as an important determinant for the functioning of firms and profit organisations, a requisite for the development of a society where paid and unpaid work will be more in balance.

The familial division of work

The French sociologist Marie-Agnès Barrère-Maurisson has developed an interesting approach to the study of the new division of labour in the family in her book 'La division familiale du travail. La vie en double' (1992). She argues that the division of work in families is 'a process which, operating simultaneously in the labour market and in the family, distributes work in accordance with the family status of individuals' (1992, p. 243). Thus an individual's position in the labour market is linked to his or her position in the family, and more broadly, his or her participation in domestic work is linked to his or her participation in paid work. The close links between the world of work and the domestic sphere mean a reinterpretation of the whole notion of work. According to the author 'work is a single entity consisting of all paid and unpaid, or domestic work' (1992, p. 116). Such a definition enables us 'to take account both of men's domestic work - and not simply of their paid work - and of all women's work, not simply that performed as part of their role within the family. It means that the family is a space in which work (both paid and unpaid) is distributed between men and women' (1992, p. 132). She concludes that, 'microsocial analysis of the familial division of labour highlights, on the one hand, different family types corresponding to particular forms of the distribution of paid and unpaid work, on the other hand, a correspondence between job and family status, i.e. a process leading to the creation of a specific division of labour. This correspondence between family and job types is also found at the macrosocial level, and particularly at that of the individual society considered in its entity' (1994, p. 10).

This new approach allows us to link the division of paid and unpaid work in the private sphere of the family to relevant developments in the societal domain. We may examine the interaction between the (re)allocation of responsibility for unpaid work in the family - and consequently the study of the forms taken by the distribution of paid work - and the (emergence of a new mode of the) distribution of work and tasks in society at large. In this respect, we want to know to what extent the (difficult) choices made by families are due to institutional (legal) forces. What role do the various social actors play in Dutch society with regard to the division of work in families? To what extent do families modify their division of paid and unpaid work as a result of policies in the field of work and family, or do they respond mainly to changing family values?

Since in many European countries the state is currently engaged in a process of shifting its responsibility to the market and the family, we have to deal with a rather complex situation. In some cases, we may observe that the actors involved have a complementary effect, in other cases their impact is more conflicting.

At present, we are not able to give a very detailed description of all the (micro and macro) factors which can explain the current division of work. Instead, we present some suggestions about the possible impact of the institutional forces and their effect on the choices made by families regarding paid and unpaid work.

Current work and family patterns

We have already noted that most of the married or cohabiting women with (young) children combine work, mostly part-time, with a high involvement in domestic tasks. Indeed, only a small number of young children (under the age of 4 years) are in child care institutions on a full-time basis. This option prevails, even among highly educated women. Their partners, after the birth of the first child, are not generally willing or are not able to reduce their working hours in order to increase their contribution to the housework and child care. In general, they maintain their full-time work schedules. Only in the public sector, do men (about 30 percent of those eligible) take parental leave and reduce their full-time workload temporarily. However, in some situations, for example after divorce, when men have to fight for custody or when they want to become actively involved with their children, they experience some of the same dilemmas as working mothers and may opt for part-time work. Apparently, the 'combination' problem is (still) mainly a female issue.

The large-scale participation of women in part-time work has facilitated the solution of two different problems: (1) the creation of paid work for women and (2) the maintenance of the active role of (one of) the parents in the education of the children. These aspects of family life in Dutch society are strongly supported by corresponding ideologies which refer respectively to the economic position of women and the preservation of traditional family values.

There is a widespread and generally accepted idea in Dutch society that women should have the same opportunities in the labour market as men. For example, the objectives of the emancipation policy, aimed at equal opportunities for men and women, are shared by many and are not particularly controversial. Only a minority of the population have serious reservations about the principle of equality and are strongly opposed to measures such as affirmative action in order to create equality and to redress the imbalance in the workforce.

At the same time we observe strong support for the idea that, if possible, children should be raised by one of the parents. Of course, this principle has never been the subject of any official debate. In former times, it was endorsed as an important basic principle in family matters. In theory, the state does not interfere in private affairs. In practice, it is sometimes different.

In fact, certain policies have important ramifications for family life, although not always as intended by the policy makers. In the absence of a well designed family policy and an adequate administration responsible for monitoring the effects of state intervention on families, we are not well informed about the impact of various state policies. Nevertheless, there are indications that some policies may have important side-effects and that, perhaps, opinions about family life will change. The following example illustrates this point.

In the last two decades, all governments in office in the Netherlands have attempted to reduce social security expenditure. The creation of and participation in paid labour has received high priority. Particularly in the nineties, (full) employment has been an important objective of state policy, as it may reduce the costs of unemployment benefits. In this respect, new legislation aimed at single mothers, has recently been introduced. The new rules force these women to accept paid work, even if they have young children. They have to rely on existing provisions for child care, which are not always available. The state will no longer guarantee the predominant position of the parents with regard to the education of their children, at least for this category of (single) parents.

It is still too early to confirm that we are facing a new trend. However, the principle of non-interference or neutrality of the state in family affairs and the lack of consideration for important side-effects of new state policies, have, in fact, not been profitable for the family. Until recently, the family has not gotten much attention in the public sphere and was not considered a matter for political concern.

This contrasts sharply with the public interest in the issue of paid labour, which in recent years has been an important target in state policies. The improvement in labour force participation of women, one of the goals of the emancipation policy, has been accompanied by various legal measures. These measures aimed at the reconciliation of work and the family, such as expansion of day care facilities, the improvement of (maternal and paternal) leave arrangements, a more flexible organisation of working hours, etc. We assume that the sharp increase in the participation rate of women with (young) children in the last twenty years is partly due to these and other labour market related measures. How the distribution of unpaid labour is affected by these policies is still a matter for consideration.

The existing ideologies, concerning the role of women in society and the recognition of the family as an important social institution, reveal some conflicting values which are largely ignored in the recent policy intervention of the state. It is possible that the (unintended) result of state intervention, in promoting the economic position of individuals, combined with shifting responsibilities from the state to other social actors, such as the family (e.g. with regard to current provisions for students and widows) may have weakened the position of the family. A tendency to rely on more solidarity in the family, in order to deal with these new responsibilities, will only be successful if the family makes use of sufficient moral and economic potentials. There is still room for the state to play an active role in various domains aimed at the well-being of the family as some experts have argued (Van den Akker, Cuyvers & De Hoog, 1992).

Future dilemmas

We have seen that the actual division of work and family is strongly associated with new dilemmas in family life. Will the future of new generations be less problematic or will families be confronted with the same difficult choices?

As the state and the market will not interfere directly in family life, a more equal division of work can only be realised if the aspirations of the family are reinforced by societal forces. The tentative results of our analysis of these forces with regard to the actual division of work have revealed the development and persistence of a gender differentiated work pattern, supported by partly conflicting ideologies and implemented in a series of state policies and agreements at lower levels (sector and company), as a result of deregulation to local authorities and social partners. The major aspects of the prevailing institutional forces with regard to the family and work patterns in Dutch society, which comprise in addition to the legal system, the underlying norms and value systems, are not directed towards a major change in this pattern. In the majority of families with young children, men will preserve their dominant position in paid work and, in spite of their progressive attitudes in favour of more equality, will not become much more active in sharing housework and child care equally. Under these circumstances we do not foresee any substantial change in the division of paid and unpaid work in the near future.

However, we have to consider the possible impact of (new) policies which may change the actual division of work to a more equal share of paid and unpaid labour between men and women and, consequently, give rise to a more relaxed family life. For the moment we lack much evidence concerning the effects of the implementation of (new) equality policies concerning the division of (unpaid) work. The analysis made by Saskia Keuzenkamp and based upon a scenario approach has shown that, according to the opinion of a group of experts, major changes in the life course of women will not occur, except to further increase their involvement in paid work. This means that more women will adopt the 'combination' model, which does not provide any real solution for the problems of the modern family, at least if men maintain their current orientation towards paid work.

Hester van der Vinne and Mascha Brink have observed that gender attitudes in favour of a more equal division of housework and child care are not (always) practised. In dealing with the question how the gap between attitudes and behaviour can be explained, they listed six types of possible clarifications for the observed inconsistency. Using data from an interview study, they tried to find out how dual-earner couples make their attitudes consistent with their behaviour. According to their conclusions the explanations that focused on restrictions (their spouse and, to a lesser extent, conflicting interests between spouses) are used most often. The explanations offered by the respondents sound very much like excuses; apparently the gap between attitudes and behaviour is closed in a verbal sense only.

In view of these results we do not expect that a move to more progressive attitudes will automatically lead to sharing family work equally. The current situation will continue as long as institutional forces 'permit' couples to maintain their unequal share in paid labour. But, we should qualify our expectations. First, new legislation, such as the introduction of a general system of 'care insurance' (Emancipatieraad, 1996) may introduce new incentives to reconsider the profits attributed to the 'combination' model. Secondly, we can not predict the unintended and unexpected consequences of institutional forces, which may arise as a result of a new balance between state and market intervention in family life, and which, consequently, may modify the current orientation towards family values.

After all, we should temper our confidence about the effects of policies on the division of paid and unpaid work. In an era where new forms of regulation of work and family will arise, for example, in the emergence of the market, social partners, and local authorities as regulatory agents, it will not be easy to identify and evaluate the impact of state intervention in this field. This means that an unambiguous assessment of the origins of new patterns of division of work in families will encounter serious theoretical and methodological problems, requiring a new research agenda. For the moment we have to admit our uncertainty about future dilemmas in family life and the ways families will deal with them. However, as the subject of a more balanced division of paid and unpaid labour remains on the political agenda, in the Netherlands as well in other European countries, strongly supported by political agencies of the European Union, there is some hope that future generations will benefit from the impact of more favourable family-work policies leading, finally, to a reallocation of paid and unpaid work within families.

References

Barrère-Maurisson, M.-A. (1992). *La division familiale du travail. La vie en double.* Paris: PUF.
Barrère-Maurisson, M.-A. (1994). *A new approach to paid and unpaid work: 'The familial division of work',* WORC Paper 94.03.005/6, Tilburg University, The Netherlands.
Emancipatieraad (1996). *Met zorg naar nieuwe zekerheid; Advies over een geëmancipeerd inkomens- en sociale zekerheid.* Den Haag.
Van den Akker, P, P. Cuyvers & C. de Hoog (1992). Gezin en overheid: de mythe van de individualisering. *Gezin, Tijdschrift voor Primaire Leefvormen. Jaargang 4, no 3-4,* 141-156.

List of tables and illustrations

List of tables and illustrations

Author index

Subject index